Lent

Proclamation 3

Aids for Interpreting
the Lessons of the Church Year

Lent

Victor Paul Furnish

Elizabeth Achtemeier, series editor

Series A

FORTRESS PRESS   Philadelphia

Library of Congress Cataloging in Publication Data

Main entry under title:

Proclamation 3.

Consists of 28 volumes in 3 series designated A, B,
and C which correspond to the cycles of the three year
lectionary. Each series contains 8 basic volumes with
the following titles: Advent-Christmas, Epiphany, Lent,
Holy Week, Easter, Pentecost 1, Pentecost 2, and
Pentecost 3.
   1. Bible—Homiletical use. 2. Bible—Liturgical
lessons, English. I. Achtemeier, Elizabeth Rice,
1926–   .
BS534.5.P765 1985   251   84–18756
ISBN 0–8006–4106–X (Series B, Pentecost 1)

2536A86   Printed in the United States of America   1–4119

Contents

Series Foreword

Proclamation 3 is an entirely new aid for preaching from the three-year ecumenical lectionary. In outward appearance this new series is similar to *Proclamation: Aids for Interpreting the Lessons of the Church Year* and *Proclamation 2*. But *Proclamation 3* has a new content as well as a new purpose.

First, there is only one author for each of the twenty-eight volumes of *Proclamation 3*. This means that each author handles both the exegesis and the exposition of the stated texts, thus eliminating the possibility of disparity between scholarly apprehension and homiletical application of the appointed lessons. While every effort was made in *Proclamation: Aids* and in *Proclamation 2* to avoid such disparity, it tended to creep in occasionally. *Proclamation 3* corrects that tendency.

Second, *Proclamation 3* is directed primarily at homiletical interpretation of the stated lessons. We have again assembled the finest biblical scholars and preachers available to write for the series; now, however, they bring their skills to us not primarily as exegetes, but as interpreters of the Word of God. Exegetical material is still presented—sometimes at length—but, most important, here it is also applied; the texts are interpreted and expounded homiletically for the church and society of our day. In this new series scholars become preachers. They no longer stand back from the biblical text and just discuss it objectively. The engage it—as the Word of God for the worshiping community. The reader therefore will not find here the divisions between "exegesis" and "homiletical interpretation" that were marked off in the two earlier series. In *Proclamation 3* the work of the pulpit is the context and goal of all that is written.

There is still some slight diversity between the several lections and calendars of the various denominations. In an effort to overcome such diversity, the North American Committee on a Common Lectionary

issued an experimental "consensus lectionary" *(The Common Lectionary)*, which is now being tried out in some congregations and
which will be further altered at the end of a three-year period. When
the final form of that lectionary appears, *Proclamation* will take
account of it. In the meantime, *Proclamation 3* deals with those texts
that are used by *most* denominations on any given Sunday. It also
continues to use the Lutheran numbering of the Sundays "after
Pentecost." But Episcopalians and Roman Catholics will find most of
their stated propers dealt with under this numbering.

Each author writes on three lessons for each Sunday, but no one
method of combining the appointed lessons has been imposed upon
the writers. The texts are sometimes treated separately, sometimes
together—according to the author's own understanding of the texts'
relationships and messages. The authors interpret the appointed texts
as these texts have spoken to them.

Victor Paul Furnish is University Distinguished Professor of New
Testament in Southern Methodist University's Perkins School of
Theology. He had two years of pastoral experience before studying at
Yale for his Ph.D. and then joining the SMU faculty. He is the author
of four books, including *2 Corinthians* in the Anchor Bible series, has
contributed to numerous other volumes including the new *Harper's
Bible Dictionary,* and is editor of the *Journal of Biblical Literature.*

Ash Wednesday

Lutheran	Roman Catholic	Episcopal	Pres/UCC/Chr	Meth/COCU
Joel 2:12–19	Joel 2:12–18	Joel 2:1–2, 12–17 or Isa. 58:1–12	Joel 2:12–18	Joel 2:12–19
2 Cor. 5:20b—6:2	2 Cor. 5:20—6:2	2 Cor. 5:20b—6:10	2 Cor. 5:20—6:2	2 Cor. 5:20b—6:10
Matt. 6:1–6, 16–21	Matt. 6:1–6, 16–18	Matt. 6:1–6, 16–21	Matt. 6:1–6, 16–18	Matt. 6:1–6, 16–21

Ash Wednesday opens the season of Lent, observed traditionally as forty days of preparation (excluding Sundays) leading up to Easter. The First Lesson appointed for reading on this opening day of the season calls us to that repentance which should lie at the heart of our preparation for Easter; the Gospel warns us about ostentatious piety; and the Second Lesson speaks of the reality of reconciliation.

FIRST LESSON: JOEL 2:12–19

The prophecies of the Book of Joel are usually dated about 400 B.C., during the period after Israel's return from exile. The second part of this book (2:28—3:21) speaks of the coming day of the Lord, and the early church found special meaning in the prophet's reference there to a future outpouring of the Spirit (2:28–29). Our text, however, comes from the first part (1:1—2:27), in which the prophet interprets some great national catastrophe as a sign of God's displeasure. Commentators are divided on the question of whether that catastrophe was literally a plague of locusts (see 1:4), or whether the devastation so vividly described here (1:11–12; 2:3; etc.) was due to an invasion of heathen armies (see 2:4–11). In either case, it is understood to be God's judgment, visited upon the people because of their transgressions. The prophet never indicates what particular transgressions he has in mind.

9

The first part of this lesson, 2:12–14, is a call to repentance, and there follow in 2:15–17 several instructions about the cultic aspects of that. The last two verses of the lesson, 2:18–19, are—within Joel itself—the opening verses of a section (2:18–27) in which the prophet is looking beyond the present disaster to a divine restoration of the nation's fortunes.

Our lesson invites reflection on several important characteristics of repentance. For one thing, repentance is to be from the heart (vv. 12, 13). This does not mean only that repentance is to be sincere, although sincerity is certainly part of it. Biblical writers characteristically identify the heart as the seat of those capacities most essential to one's being human. One's deepest emotions, profoundest thoughts, and most authentic moral commitments are all centered there. Moreover, it is through the heart that one approaches, and is approached by, God. Thus to "return to [God] with all [of one's] heart" requires a fundamental reorientation of one's whole being—every faculty responsive to God's presence and to God's will, nothing withheld. The prophet does not dispute that things like fasting, weeping, and mourning may be appropriate signs of repentance (v. 12). He does not identify them with the substance of it, however. Only when one's life has been opened up to God (the torn heart of v. 13a) has repentance really taken place.

Repentance, however, although it is always to be from the heart, is never simply a matter of personal decision and commitment. Here is a second point that this text calls to our attention: true repentance necessarily has a corporate as well as an individual dimension. Israel's disobedience was something more than the sum of the personal transgressions of numerous individuals, so the prophet's appeals are directed to the nation as a whole, to Zion (v. 15). To return to God means a return to being God's people, a return to one another within a community of faith. Therefore, in vv. 15–17 the prophet calls Israel to a communal act of repentance, the great urgency of which requires an interruption of the normal course of affairs—even the nursing of an infant and the consummation of a marriage. At the "solemn assembly" to which all are summoned (vv. 15–16) the supplications of the priests are for the people as a whole (v. 17), because they stand together before their God. Repentance, unquestionably, is a personal matter, since it requires the wholehearted commitment of the individual; but it is not a private matter. It is within the community that the call to repent is received and that repentance takes place, because the heart that has been opened to God has also been opened to others.

A third point is of absolutely fundamental importance. This lection reminds us that repentance in the biblical sense involves the renewal of one's trust in God. Confessing one's sin and promising to do better does not amount to repentance, no matter how profound one's sense of guilt or how sincere one's resolve to change. Indeed, insofar as this resolve presumes an ability to reform oneself, it represents a hardening of the heart, not an opening of it to God and to others. But no such presumption is involved in our text. Quite the contrary, our text presupposes one's need for God, even as it emphasizes God's caring and compassion. Thus, at the very center of the prophet's summons to repentance is his affirmation of a God who "is gracious and merciful, slow to anger, and abounding in steadfast love, and repents of evil" (v. 13).

This affirmation derives, ultimately, from the Yahwist's understanding of God as that is expressed in Exod. 34:6–7. Moses, on Mount Sinai, discovers that the Lord is "a God merciful and gracious, slow to anger, and abounding in steadfast love for thousands, forgiving iniquity and transgression and sin, but who will by no means clear the guilty. . . . " This perception, found as well in many other Old Testament passages (for example, Num. 14:18; Neh. 9:17, 31; Pss. 86:15; 103:8; Jer. 32:18), is fundamental to Israel's sense of being a covenant people, absolutely accountable to a God who is just but also full of compassion, faithful to them even when they are unfaithful. It is this old Yahwistic formula about God's mercy that is used to support the appeal in Joel 2:13. The prophet understands that repentance involves both a confession of one's need for mercy and a confession of faith in a just and compassionate God.

Finally, this passage can help us recognize that repentance as such does not effect salvation, nor does it entitle us to receive it. Salvation is from God, at God's good pleasure, an expression of God's free and gracious choosing to save. This conviction finds expression when the prophet, like the tradition before him, speaks of the possibility of God's "repenting" of the evil that has been visited upon Israel (v. 13;

see Jer. 18:7–8; 26:3, 13, 19; 42:10; Exod. 32:12, 14; 2 Sam. 24:16; Jon. 4:2); while the call to repentance presumes that God is gracious and slow to anger, it does not presume that God's compassion can be coerced. It is significant that v. 14 is posed as a question: "Who knows whether [Gᴄ ˙] will not turn and repent, and leave a blessing behind him, a cereal offering and a drink offering for the Lord, your God?" (see also Jon. 3:9a). Even as the prophet affirms the possibility of forgiveness and blessing, he is warning Israel that God remains free to grant or to withhold these. The point is that repentance, even when it is genuine, provides no guarantee; nothing that we do can warrant God's love. God alone warrants that, for love cannot be earned or coerced. Where repentance is followed by a blessing, that comes as a gift, not as a reward.

The material blessings our lection has in view—the cereal and drink offerings provided for worship (v. 14), and the return of a plentiful harvest (vv. 18–19)—are understood as tokens of the love and compassion of a gracious God, not as benefits to which Israel is entitled by reason of her repentance. Such blessings are, in fact, not only *from* God, but *"for* the Lord, your God" (v. 14). Their bestowal does not mean that an account has been closed, but that an account has been opened that will never be closed; for the blessing that is received by those who have heeded the call to repent involves a new call—to a stewardship of the gifts of God.

SECOND LESSON: 2 CORINTHIANS 5:20b—6:2

It is likely that our canonical 2 Corinthians combines two originally separate letters of Paul to his Corinthian congregation, the earlier of these represented by chapters 1–9, and the later represented by chapters 10–13. The earlier, from which this passage is taken, may be divided into three main sections, each of which corresponds to one of the apostle's primary reasons for writing: *(a)* earnest assurances that, despite the doubts of some, he really does care about his congregation in Corinth, 1:12—2:13; *(b)* an exposition of his understanding of apostleship and, in particular, of what he understands his own apostleship to mean for his readers, 2:14—5:19; and *(c)* a series of appeals—to be reconciled with God, 5:20—6:10; to be reconciled with Paul, their apostle, 6:11—7:3; and to follow through on their previous commitment to make a contribution to the collection that he has obligated himself to take to the church in Jerusalem, 7:4—9:15.

The theme of our lection, therefore, is reconciliation, and in form it is an appeal. Although the language and the historical setting of this appeal are different, it is fundamentally the same as the call to "return to the Lord" in the First Lesson (Joel 2:13). Still, it is worth noticing that the apostle, even more explicitly than the prophet, bases his appeal on the certainty that salvation is a gift from God, a result of God's purpose and not of one's own decision to "return." Specifically, the appeal in 2 Cor. 5:20—6:2 has to be interpreted in the light of the affirmation in 5:18–19, to which it is closely tied: In Christ God has reconciled us to himself, not holding our trespasses against us, and establishing among us the ministry and message of reconciliation. Here Paul has drawn on a traditional statement about reconciliation (v. 19ab) to help him formulate his interpretation of the meaning of the creedal affirmation about Christ's saving death upon which he had drawn a few sentences earlier (vv. 14–15).

The juxtaposition of affirmation and appeal that we see here reflects the apostle's conviction that God's gift of salvation always involves a claim. It is not that the gift is conditional upon one's acknowledging the claim, for then it would not be a gift. Rather, Paul believes that the claim inheres in the gift, so when the gift is bestowed a claim is made. Thus, in this passage the appeal to "be reconciled" (5:20b) presupposes the affirmation that in Christ one's reconciliation has already been effected. That the apostle formulates this appeal in the passive voice (he does not say, "Reconcile yourselves"!) is a further indication that here, as elsewhere in his letters, indicative and imperative are profoundly related.

The appeal to be reconciled to God is followed by an assertion about Christ's atoning work (5:21), probably Paul's reworking of a Jewish-Christian formula. The influence of Second Isaiah's portrait of the Suffering Servant is apparent when Christ is described as one who was "made . . . to be sin" although he himself "knew no sin" (see Isa. 53:6, 9). That is, although Christ himself was not a sinner, the burden of the sins of others was laid upon him in order that they "might become the righteousness of God." By recapitulating, although in different language, what had been affirmed about the reality of a new creation and reconciliation in 5:17–19, this declaration about a startling exchange of sin and righteousness helps to support the appeal of 5:20b. The apostle believes that one can indeed be reconciled to God, because reconciliation is already established in Christ. Moreover, while he incorporates a traditional saying about God's "not counting" the world's sin against it (5:19ab), one can see that for Paul himself reconciliation means something far more than that. It means participating in the reality of a new creation (5:17), and becoming a new person in Christ—becoming, in fact, "the righteousness of God" (5:21).

To the appeal of 5:20b a second is added in 6:1, "not to accept the grace of God in vain." Here Paul is thinking of the gospel of God's grace as he had proclaimed it in Corinth, and his plea is that those whom he has won over to Christ remain faithful to that gospel. Although the apostle professes complete confidence in the Corinthians (7:16), he is aware that some of them have not fully understood his priorities in ministry (see, for example, 1:12—2:13; 5:11–13; 6:3). The present appeal reflects his concern about this, and shows that the apostle's call for his readers to be reconciled to God is closely related to his call for them to be reconciled to his own apostolate (the focus in 6:11—7:3). In 6:3–10 Paul supports his appeal by contending that, despite claims to the contrary, the unheroic character of his ministry has not hindered the gospel and should not be faulted, but is fully appropriate to his service as a servant of God.

The concluding verse of our lection (6:2), again formulated as an indicative, supports everything that has been said in 5:20—6:1. Paul first quotes Isa. 49:8a, which speaks of "the acceptable time" (or: "the time of favor") and "the day of salvation." In the context of Second Isaiah these phrases describe the prophet's own day, when Jerusalem is comforted with the assurance that God has "listened" to her cries and has pardoned her iniquity (see Isa. 40:1–2). Paul, however, gives the text a broader and specifically Christian meaning. For him, the "day of salvation" refers to more than God's pardoning of a particular people at a particular time in history. When he declares that this day is "now" (6:2b), he is thinking of the reality of the "new creation" given in Christ (5:17), of God's reconciling of the world to himself (5:19), and of the gift of righteousness (5:21).

In the First Lesson appointed for reading on this Ash Wednesday, the prophet calls Israel to "return" to God, confident that God's mercy and love are never withdrawn. In the Second Lesson the apostle calls his Corinthian congregation to "be reconciled" to God, confident that reconciliation has already been effected in Christ. In both texts there is an emphasis on the present as a time for commitment: "'Yet even now,' says the Lord, 'return to me with all your heart . . .'" (Joel 2:12); "Behold, now is the acceptable time; behold, now is the day of salvation" (2 Cor. 6:2b). Neither the prophet nor the apostle allows us to linger in contemplation of our sins, any more than the evangelist allows us to indulge in the sanctimonious display of our sorrow for them (Matt. 6:16–18). These texts remind us that on Ash Wednesday the gospel is still the gospel—the good news of a love that will not let us go.

GOSPEL: MATTHEW 6:1–6, 16–21

In the Sermon on the Mount from which these verses are drawn, the author of the Gospel of Matthew has put together, in accord with his own point of view and intentions, a number of diverse sayings that the church of his day (a date in the 80s seems likely) attributed to Jesus. The opening verse of this lection would appear to be the evangelist's own heading for the materials that follow in vv. 2–18. The verses that close the lection (vv. 19–21) properly belong to the next section of the Sermon where the topics are, first, possessions (vv. 19–24) and then, closely related to that, anxiety (vv. 25–34).

The word often translated as "piety" in v. 1 (so, e.g., the RSV) is the same one rendered as "righteousness" in most other passages. Righteousness is, to be sure, a major theme both in this Gospel as a whole and specifically in chapters 5–7. In our passage, however, the word has a narrower reference, for it is clear that the evangelist is thinking of the specific religious exercises about which comments are made in the following paragraphs (vv. 2–18). He sums up the point of these comments in his warning to avoid any ostentatious display of one's piety. Pious practices themselves are not criticized, but only doing them in order to win for oneself the admiration of other people. It would appear that the evangelist has in mind the kind of pretentious piety of which he accuses "the Pharisees" in 23:5: "They do all their

deeds to be seen by men. . . . '' The warning here in 6:1 is that if one
seeks the reward for one's piety from the world, one is thereby giving
up the only lasting reward, which is the one that comes from God.

This contrast between worldly and heavenly rewards is continued
in the following verses, where three examples of pious acts are given:
almsgiving (vv. 2–4), prayer (vv. 5–6), and fasting (vv. 16–18). Although these are not specifically commanded in the Mosaic law, they
were often commended in Jewish teaching—as, for example, in the
declaration of Tob. 12:8 that "prayer is good when accompanied by
fasting, almsgiving, and righteousness.'' Except for the Lord's Prayer
(vv. 9–13), which the evangelist found appropriate to include in this
context, there are no parallels to vv. 2–18 in the other Gospels.

When the Lord's Prayer and vv. 7–8 which introduce it are
bracketed out, as our lection appropriately does, one can readily see
that the comments on almsgiving, prayer, and fasting exhibit the same
structural pattern: (1) An introductory phrase ("And when you . . . ,''
vv. 2a, 5a, 16a) presumes that the pious practice named is perfectly
legitimate. (2) A condemnation of hypocrisy (vv. 2b, 5b, 16b) presumes that some perform it only to win the admiration of others. (3) A
statement beginning with "truly" (vv. 2c, 5c, 16c) emphasizes that
those who have been praised for their piety by human beings will have
no further reward. (4) An appeal to avoid the display of one's piety
(vv. 3–4a, 6a, 17–18a) is supported by the promise of a higher reward
(vv. 4b, 6b, 18b).

Almsgiving (vv. 2–4) included various kinds of charitable deeds
performed to aid the poor and the destitute, and this evangelist—far
from criticizing it—clearly regards such activity as required by the
superior righteousness (5:20) to which Jesus had summoned his followers (see especially the parable of the last judgment, 25:31–46).
Similarly, in vv. 5–6 it is not prayer as such that is being criticized, nor
public prayer specifically. The criticism is directed at those who pray
because they want to be seen praying, rather than because of their
genuine devotion to God.

Fasting (vv. 16–18) was another special religious activity, practiced
by pious Jews twice a week (see Luke 18:12) and ordinarily accompanied by smearing ashes over one's body and wearing sackcloth,
both as signs of penitence. Even though this evangelist, like the

authors of Mark and Luke, knows the tradition that Jesus had not enjoined his disciples to fast (Matt. 9:14–15 and parallels), the propriety of fasting is not the issue in this present passage. The issue is why and how one fasts, and once more the criticism is of those who want only to demonstrate their piety to the world. The point is emphasized by a play on words which can only be paraphrased in English ("disfigure their faces" and "may be seen" in v. 16 are formed from the same Greek verb).

In each of these cases, those who are criticized for making a show of their religious devotion are identified as "hypocrites." This term derives from the Greek theater where it was used of the actors—people who played roles for others to see. It is a favorite Matthean word, occurring most often in chapter 23 where it describes those ("Pharisees") who strive for the appearance of righteousness without attending to the substance of it (thus, 23:28). In our lection (vv. 2, 5, 16) the original reference of "hypocrite" to a public "role-player" comes through very clearly. The point is that true piety does not seek the limelight, does not parade itself before the world. It operates "in secret" (vv. 4, 6, 18), which means out of devotion to God and not out of a need for public approval. Thus, piety's true reward comes from "your Father who sees in secret" (vv. 4, 6, 18); it inheres in the relationship between the pious and their God, to which every genuine act of piety is itself a response.

What more provocative passage could be read in a congregation assembled on Ash Wednesday for the imposition of ashes? How can worshipers be invited to receive the mark of the cross on their foreheads—and to leave it displayed there throughout the day—when this lection seems to call for secret devotions, and even a scrubbed face (v. 17)? Indeed, this text properly warns that any good work or devotional act can easily become an occasion for ostentatious self-display. The point, however, is not that all benefactions should be made anonymously, and that prayer and fasting must always be conducted in private. It is, rather, that no charitable deed or religious exercise is truly righteous if it is motivated simply by the desire to be noticed and commended by others. A public witness to one's faith is certainly not ruled out, and it is even emphasized in the distinctively Matthean saying found earlier in this same discourse: "Let your light

so shine before men, that they may see your good works and give glory
to your Father who is in heaven" (5:16). This evangelist recognizes
that the public display of good works has the character of public
witness when one's goal is the greater glory of God, and that is what is
called for in Matt. 5:16. He also recognizes, however, that when the
goal is to bring honor upon oneself, witness yields to hypocrisy—and
that is what is condemned in 6:1-18.

The First Sunday in Lent

Lutheran	Roman Catholic	Episcopal	Pres/UCC/Chr	Meth/COCU
Gen. 2:7–9, 15–17; 3:1–7	Gen. 2:7–9; 3:1–7	Gen. 2:4b–9, 15–17, 25—3:7	Gen. 2:7–9; 3:1–7	Gen. 2:4b–9, 15–17, 25; 3:1–7
Rom. 5:12 (13–16) 17–19	Rom. 5:12–19 or Rom. 5:12, 17–19	Rom. 5:12–19 (20–21)	Rom. 5:12–19	Rom. 5:12–21
Matt. 4:1–11	Matt. 4:1–11	Matt. 4:1–11	Matt. 4:1–1 i	Matt. 4:1–11

The First Lesson for this Sunday probes the meaning of temptation
and disobedience; the Second Lesson declares that Christ's life-giving
act of righteousness overcomes sin and death; and the Gospel tells us
how Jesus was tempted but did not yield to temptation.

FIRST LESSON:
GENESIS 2:7–9, 15–17; 3:1–7

The verses that comprise this lection are taken from a creation
account that opens at Gen. 2:4b and extends through chapter 3. This
particular account is ordinarily attributed to a tenth-century B.C.
narrative source that has come to be described as "Yahwist," because
in it God is known by the proper name Yahweh. In sharp contrast to
the much later Priestly account in Gen. 1:1—2:4a, this Yahwist narrative shows little interest in the creation of "the heavens and the earth"
(Gen. 1:1; 2:4a). Rather, all of the attention is focused on the creation
of humanity and on humanity's relationship to God. Thus, the opening

verses (2:4b–6) are only preliminary to the description of the Lord's formation of a man (v. 7) with which our lection begins. Verses 10–14 of chapter 2 represent a digression within the narrative itself, and nothing very important is lost by their omission from the lection. It is important, however, to take some account of what is said in 2:18–25 about the creation of a woman, because she is prominent in 3:1–7; and the encounter between this couple and the Lord (3:8–24) must also be kept in view.

In contrast with the majestic declaration of the Priestly account, that "God created man in his own image" (1:27), we have in 2:7 a rather intimate description of the creative act itself. Carefully, almost tenderly, the Lord shapes a little figure from the moistened earth and breathes life into it. From the very first, then, our attention is drawn to the relationship that exists between the Creator and the human being. God's breath, it must be stressed, does not reside in the man as a separate entity, as a "soul," but enlivens the whole body.

The Lord's care for this living being is also demonstrated when the man is placed within "Eden" (the Hebrew word *eden* means "bliss"), 2:8. It is described as a park (RSV: "garden") full of trees, 2:9, and it makes one think of nothing so much as the spacious grounds of a royal palace. The remark that the Lord "put [the man] in the garden of Eden to till it and keep it" (2:15) should not be overlooked. First, this note informs us that labor was already part of the man's life before the Fall. Thus, we are not to understand the punishment for his disobeying God (described in 3:17–19) as "having to work." His punishment is, rather, experiencing work as a burden, as meaningless toil without good result. Second, the man's proper work is understood to be as the caretaker and steward of God's creation—protecting it (to "keep it") even while he is developing its resources ("to till it"). Neither the fragility of nature nor the difficulty in simultaneously enjoying and conserving it is the topic here, but the principle is nonetheless clear and compelling: God's good gifts are to be used but not exploited.

Two of the trees in this park are identified in 2:9 as having a special status, "the tree of life" and "the tree of the knowledge of good and evil." Only one special tree is mentioned in the remainder of the narrative, however (2:17; 3:3–16, 22–24), so it is likely that two separate traditions have been combined, and that "the tree of life" and "the tree of the knowledge of good and evil" are actually one and the same. The Lord's commandment putting this one tree off-limits to the groundskeeper (2:17) is a reminder that the man lives and labors in the park at the pleasure of the Creator. Moreover, because the man is responsible for obeying this commandment, a moral factor has been introduced. The "knowledge of good and evil" is to be understood in the comprehensive sense of an omniscience like God's. Therefore, to eat of the forbidden fruit would be to transgress the boundary line between the man's status and God's—a violation not only of God's commandment, but of the groundskeeper's own humanity.

Two points are worth noting about vv. 18–25, even though they are omitted from the present lection. First, the man that the Lord has brought into being and endowed with life remains the object of his Creator's attention and concern: "It is not good that the man should be alone" (2:18). Second, the woman who becomes the man's partner and companion is created as his equal, fully sharing his humanity ("bone of my bones and flesh of my flesh," 2:23). Thus, when the woman falls prey to temptation and eats of the fruit of the forbidden tree (3:1–6), it is not because she is the weaker of the two human beings. She, like the man who eats with her, represents the whole of humanity.

It is with this story of temptation and disobedience that our lection concludes. The purpose of the narrative is not to explain the origin of evil but to explore the nature and meaning of the disobedience into which humanity has fallen. The serpent is itself one of God's creatures (3:1), and is not identified as a satanic figure or as the cause of humanity's downfall. Its role in the narrative is primarily to provide the occasion for a dialogue, in the course of which two significant insights into the nature of the human predicament emerge.

First, that predicament begins with the attempt to blunt the force of the divine commandment. Although the woman corrects the serpent's suggestion that the fruit of all of Eden's trees had been placed off-limits (3:1–2), to the commandment about the one tree she herself adds the words: "Neither shall you touch it" (3:3). It might appear, on the surface, that this addition strengthens the Lord's commandment; but actually, by interposing a rule of her own in order to play it safe, the woman is distancing herself from the real commandment and trying to play God. How often have we, too, yielded to this temptation? How often have we sought to claim divine authority for moral rules and duties of our own devising? And how often have we clung to them, not really to honor God, but to avoid God's own more radical commandment?

Second, the essence of disobedience is portrayed here as humanity's striving to "be like God, knowing good and evil" (3:5), a yearning to be "wise" (3:6) as God alone can be wise, a wanting to be independent of God and autonomous. This above all is what attracts the woman to the forbidden fruit and prompts her to share it with her companion; but the result is not what they had anticipated. The knowledge they gain neither ennobles their life nor gives them control over it, but leads only to shame (3:7) and grief (3:14–19).

This First Lesson includes no call to repentance, conveys no word of pardon, offers no promise of deliverance. What it does offer is a vivid but also nuanced portrayal of the human condition, and along with that a sobering insight into the nature of the human predicament. It is to this condition and this predicament that the Second Lesson is directly addressed.

SECOND LESSON:
ROMANS 5:12 (13–16) 17–19

The story of Genesis 3 is directly in view in this Second Lesson, and it is important to notice how Paul reads it and responds to it. First, however, one must take account of the character of Romans, and of how these verses fit into the apostle's argument as it has been developing since 3:21.

In this letter the apostle comes closer than in any other to providing a comprehensive exposition of his understanding of the gospel. This is due partly to the fact that Romans is addressed to a church that he had not founded, so that in advance of his first visit he needs to introduce himself and the gospel he preaches. It may be due even more, however, to the fact that the apostle is writing on the eve of his departure (from Corinth) with an offering for the Christians of Jerusalem (see Rom. 15:14–32). Because, by prior agreement with the elders of the Jerusalem church (see Gal. 2:9–10), this has been collected from Paul's gentile congregations, it is a token of his whole ministry—and thus of his whole understanding of the gospel. How it will be received and how he himself will be received may very well be the questions uppermost in his mind as he writes. Therefore, we find Paul, as if in preparation for some crucial discussions in Jerusalem, seriously reflecting on issues of absolutely fundamental theological importance.

In the section of the letter from which our lection has been drawn Paul's reflections center on the righteousness of God. The thesis first affirmed in 1:16–17, that righteousness comes as a gift from God to those who live by faith, is restated in 3:21–26 and then variously elaborated in what follows, especially through chapter 5. It is important to notice, however, that the argument in this part of the letter builds on the comments in 1:18—3:20 about humanity's plight, estranged from God and subject to God's wrath. Indeed, the thesis of the earlier discussion is formulated most succinctly in 3:22b–23, precisely as the discussion of God's righteousness is opening: "There is no distinction [between Jew and Gentile]; since all have sinned and fall short of the glory of God."

The argument of the immediate context is governed by the affirmation of 5:1, that "since we are justified by faith, we have peace with God through our Lord Jesus Christ." In vv. 6–11 the decisive saving event is identified as Christ's death, whereby God's love has justified, reconciled, and given life to those who otherwise—in their weakness, ungodliness, and sinfulness—remain God's enemies. In order to emphasize the wonder of this, Paul goes on in vv. 12–21 to contrast Adam's legacy of sin and death with the free gift of God's grace bestowed in Christ. There is no specific citation of or quotation from Genesis 3, but that narrative lies very much in the background of the discussion here.

Paul is emphasizing just one main point in this pericope: If death has become the destiny of the whole of humanity because of one man's act of disobedience, how much more will life be given through the obedience of Jesus Christ. Here a familiar rabbinic pattern of argumentation is being followed ("from the lesser to the greater")—if (the lesser figure) Adam could have brought so much death, then (the greater figure) Christ must be able to bring an abundance of life. The apostle begins this line of argument in v. 12, but the sentence is never completed. Instead, he digresses in vv. 13–14 to comment on the law's role in bringing sin and death (a subject already broached in 3:20 and 4:15). Thus, so far as the main point of the passage is concerned it makes sense to designate vv. 13–14 as parenthetical. This cannot be said of vv. 15–16, however, because here Paul's thesis finds its first complete statement. It is then restated—with certain variations and elaborations—not just once, but three times in quick succession: in v. 17, again in v. 18, and yet again in v. 19. The last two verses of the pericope are omitted from the lection, perhaps because the topic of the law is taken up once more in v. 20 (compare vv. 13–14). Still, the main point of the passage is not abandoned, but in fact reformulated in v. 21 for one last time.

The personal name "Adam" derives from a Hebrew word *(adham)* which was used of humanity in general, as well as of individual (male) persons. While Paul is certainly thinking of Adam as that "one man" (vv. 12, 17, 18, 19) who disobeyed God's commandment in Eden, he clearly regards him as representative—indeed, as inclusive—of all of humanity (note the reference to "all men" in v. 18). His existence is characterized by sin and death, by a fundamental alienation from the God whose claim he has refused to acknowledge. Adam's plight is therefore the human plight, on which Paul has already discoursed at some length in this letter (1:18—3:20). Now, however, he wants to stress Christ's act of obedience that leads to righteousness and life, not Adam's act of disobedience that leads to sin and death. These two figures are set over against one another in a similar way in 1 Cor. 15:21–22, and in 1 Cor. 15:45 the apostle even writes of Christ as "the last Adam."

In using this as a Lenten text, it may be advisable to put vv. 13–14 and 20–21 aside. To say anything about them would necessarily involve an exposition of Paul's important but complex idea of how the law actually produces transgression. Moreover, because the apostle makes a special point of the fact that the law came in only with Moses (vv. 13–14), it is apparent that he does not see obedience to the law as an issue in the story of the Fall. One might suggest that the issue the story does raise for Paul—and for us—is the nature of God. Has the God who tenderly formed the man from clay and breathed life into his nostrils, who granted him the pleasures and satisfactions of life in Eden, and who, concerned for the loneliness of his existence there,

brought forth a woman to be his companion—has this God finally
abandoned humanity to sin and death? In Rom. 5:12–21 Paul is saying,
no! How much greater than Adam's disobedience is God's grace! How
much greater than Adam's burden of sin and death is God's gift, in
Christ, of righteousness and life! What Paul means by the "righteousness" and "life" that come in Christ has been suggested in 5:1–11 (see
also Rom. 6:1—7:6 and chapter 8)—reconciliation with God, and thus
the restoration of one's own true humanity.

As the thesis of this passage is stated and restated, one particular
point is emphasized: the righteousness that allows us to "reign in life
through the one man Jesus Christ" comes to us from God as an
absolutely "free gift" (vv. 15, 16, 17). This is why Christ's obedience
is "much greater" than Adam's disobedience. While sin is a human
act of defiant self-assertion, earning death as its "wages," the righteousness by which life is constituted as "eternal" is an act of divine
grace, bestowed apart from any human deserving (see 5:21; 6:23).
Even as the apostle, with a view to Genesis 3, acknowledges the
seriousness of humanity's estrangement from God, he is affirming the
reality of God's grace as that is freely offered in Christ for righteousness and for life.

GOSPEL: MATTHEW 4:1–11

In the Gospel for this Sunday, as in the First Lesson, we have a story
in which the experience of temptation plays an important role.
Moreover, in both stories the temptation is to be like God. The
outcome here is different, of course, because this narrative is not
about humanity's estrangement from God, but about Jesus "the Son of
God" (vv. 3, 6). One must therefore recognize from the outset that the
evangelist's intention is not to portray humanity's common predicament (so the Yahwist in Genesis 3), or to affirm how by God's grace
that has been overcome (so Paul in Romans 5). Rather, his intention is
to show that this Jesus truly is God's Son, as a heavenly voice had
declared him to be at his baptism (3:17), and that instead of yielding to
the temptation to usurp God's power, he placed his absolute and
unwavering trust in God.

From the comments in Heb. 2:18 ("For because [Jesus] himself has
suffered and been tempted, he is able to help those who are tempted")

and 4:15 ("For we have . . . a high priest . . . who in every respect has been tempted as we are, yet without sinning"), it would appear that a tradition about Jesus' temptation was well established in the church, and played a role in its christology. The earliest narrative account of Jesus undergoing temptation is probably the brief notice in Mark 1:12–13 which provides us only with a setting for it (in the wilderness, with the wild beasts and ministering angels), its duration (over a period of forty days), and its source ("Satan"). The substantially enlarged accounts that we find here in Matthew and in Luke 4:1–13 are usually regarded as deriving from the hypothetical source Q, although each of the evangelists has altered that in his own distinctive way. It is clear that the narrative, which must have originated in the post-Easter church, seeks to draw parallels between Jesus' experience and the experiences of the Israelites during their forty years of wandering in the wilderness (see Exod. 12:37—17:16; Num. 11—14; etc.).

Within the overall plan of Matthew, this narrative stands among those that portray Jesus preparing for his ministry. It follows directly on the account of Jesus' baptism, as it also does in Mark (but not in Luke, where a long genealogy intervenes). Three distinctively Matthean touches should be noted in the way the story is introduced (vv. 1–2). First, only this evangelist describes Jesus as "fasting" in the wilderness, using the cultic term; Mark had attributed no motive to his being there, whereas Luke simply says that "he ate nothing" (Luke 4:2). Second, whereas both Mark and Luke refer to "forty days" in the wilderness, Matthew adds, "and forty nights," presumably to draw a parallel with Moses' fasting on Mount Sinai (Exod. 34:28). Third, only in this Matthean account is it said that Jesus was in the wilderness "to be"—that is, *in order* "to be tempted by the devil." Guided by the Spirit, Jesus seems actually to be inviting a confrontation with evil—a confrontation that will demonstrate that he is truly God's Son.

The bulk of the story consists of a dialogue in which we find even the devil quoting Scripture as, three times, he tries to tempt Jesus. The first temptation (vv. 3–4) is for Jesus to prove his divine Sonship by performing a miracle. But, as in 12:38–42 (parallel in Luke 11:29–32) and 16:1–4 (parallel in Mark 8:11–12), no miracle is granted. Instead, Jesus quotes Deut. 8:3b, drawn from Moses' reminder to the Israelites that when they hungered in the wilderness God met their needs. In this response to the devil's call for a miracle, we are to see that Jesus' Sonship does not consist in his power to do extraordinary things, like turning stones to bread. Whether Jesus could have done this is not the issue, for both the tradition and this evangelist undoubtedly presumed that he could. The point is that his divine Sonship is not thereby demonstrated. What demonstrates that is his absolute trust in God, and this is what the quotation from Deuteronomy is meant to convey.

Although Jesus had been led into the wilderness by the Spirit (v. 1), it is the devil who transports him from there to Jerusalem, which is the setting for the second temptation (vv. 5–7). The devil still wants proof of Jesus' Sonship, but now he takes a somewhat different approach, suddenly appearing to be very pious. If, as the first response has suggested, Jesus' trust in God demonstrates that he is God's Son, then let him prove how much he trusts God—and, indeed, how trustworthy his God is! Quoting a scriptural assurance that God will protect those who trust in God (Ps. 91:11–12), the devil challenges Jesus to take a literal "leap of faith" from atop the temple. Jesus once more resists, and counters the devil's text with one of his own: "You shall not tempt the Lord your God." This admonition has been quoted from Deut. 6:16, but for its context one must consult Exod. 17:1–7, where the Israelites are said to have faulted Moses—and therefore God—for having provided no water in the desert (v. 2). Their complaint is interpreted in Exod. 17:7 as a test of whether God is really present with them. Similarly, the devil is wanting proof that the God in whom Jesus trusts really is present with him, and the issue is whether by trusting in God fully enough one can presume upon God's will and power to save.

For the final temptation (vv. 8–10) the devil transports Jesus "to a very high mountain." This could be the evangelist's own touch, since he is fond of providing mountaintop settings for important teachings (chapters 5–7 and 28:16–20 are examples that have no parallels in Mark or Luke). Clearly, we have come to the climactic point in the present narrative. Now Jesus is offered the kingdoms of the world and their glory if he will abandon God and worship the devil. There is not even the pretense of piety here, but a bribe, pure and simple. To resist this temptation will necessarily involve rejecting the tempter himself, and that is exactly what Jesus does—with a sharp, "Begone Satan!" (perhaps anticipating the rebuke of Peter at Caesarea Philippi, 16:23), and a quotation of the commandment to worship no other God but the Lord (Deut. 6:13). Thus, the conclusion in v. 11 mentions not only the angels who come to minister to Jesus (probably drawn from the Markan version), but the devil's departure; Jesus has confronted temptation and overcome it.

In the first two cases Jesus has been tempted to exploit his relationship to God by bringing God's power under his own control; and to have submitted to either temptation would have amounted to the refusal to let God be God—which is precisely the point of the third temptation. Here the story of Genesis 3 has been played out again, but with new actors and a different conclusion. The one is a story about humanity's disobedience and alienation from God, while the other is a story about Jesus' perfect obedience and divine Sonship. In Romans 5 these two themes come together as Paul affirms that Christ's act of obedience (in the cross) is humanity's salvation.

The Second Sunday in Lent

Lutheran	Roman Catholic	Episcopal	Pres/UCC/Chr	Meth/COCU
Gen. 12:1–8	Gen. 12:1–4	Gen. 12:1–8	Gen. 12:1–7	Gen. 12:1–8
Rom. 4:1–5, 13–17	2 Tim. 1:8b–10	Rom. 4:1–5 (6–12) 13–17	2 Tim. 1:8–14	Rom. 4:1–17
John 4:5–26 (27–30, 39–42)	Matt. 17:1–9	John 3:1–17	Matt. 17:1–9	John 4:5–26

The First Lesson tells of God's promise to Abraham concerning his descendants, of Abraham's departure for the land of Canaan, and of God's further promise once he has arrived there. The excerpts from Romans 4 that comprise the Second Lesson offer comments on the faith that characterized Abraham's receipt of those promises. Abraham and his line also figure in the Gospel lection, even though indirectly; the story of Jesus' conversation with the Samaritan woman is set at a well named for one of Abraham's grandsons and close by a piece of family property. However, at a deeper level the common theme of these three lections is not Abraham and his descendants, but God and God's promise of life. It is this theme in particular that should be kept in mind as one reflects on these readings for the Second Sunday in Lent.

FIRST LESSON: GENESIS 12:1-9

This passage, like the one from Genesis assigned for the First Sunday in Lent, is ordinarily attributed to the tenth-century B.C. Yahwist source. The name "Abram," used throughout Gen. 11:26—17:24, is perhaps a shortened form of "Abiram," of which "Abraham" is probably an Aramaic expansion. The reader has already learned that Abram was one of three sons of Terah (Gen. 11:26), that Abram took Sarai (Sarah) as his wife (11:29), and that Sarai's womb was barren (11:30). One now reads in Gen. 12:1-3 about the Lord's call of Abram, and in 12:4-8 about Abram's departure for and arrival in Canaan. Although the lection ends with v. 8, one might well argue that the pericope itself ends only with the note in v. 9 about Abram's continuing journey toward the Negeb.

Beginning here in chapter 12 the focus of the narratives in Genesis shifts from universal (or "primeval") history—the history of humanity in general—to the history of Israel in particular. This narrowing of focus had already commenced with the genealogy of Gen. 11:10-26, which starts with Noah's son Shem and traces that line down to Terah's three sons, Abram, Nahor, and Haran. Still, one is hardly prepared for the apparently arbitrary singling out of Abram by the Lord which is portrayed in Gen. 12:1-3—"Now the Lord said to Abram . . ." Why Abram? This question is neither posed nor answered. The important thing to notice is that the narrator understands Israel's history to have been, from the very beginning, the history of God's dealing with an elect people, and their response to God's coming and call.

In the case of Abram, the Lord's call is a very radical one indeed. He is summoned to give up those connections that are ordinarily regarded as most crucial for establishing a person's identity: his country, his clan (the wider circle of kinfolk), and his immediate family (v. 1). He is called to go forth to a new land according to the Lord's direction—in effect, to receive a new identity. No one can heed such a call without trusting completely in the one who has called, a point not missed by the Christian author who writes of the "faith" in which Abraham "went out, not knowing where he was to go," but only that God's "promise" was sure (Heb. 11:8–10).

God's first promise to Abram is specified in vv. 2–3, and it is threefold. First, he will have many descendants, thereby becoming the father of a great nation (see also Gen 13:16; 15:5; 17:5–6; 22:17; 26:24; 35:11; etc.). Second, his "name" will be made great, that is, his line will be renowned among the nations. Here there is perhaps an allusion to the story of the tower of Babel, whose builders had sought to "make a name" for themselves (Gen. 11:4). What they had vainly sought to achieve by their own efforts, the Lord will freely grant to Abram's descendants. Third, the Lord promises that Abram "will be a blessing" to "all the families of the earth." What that may entail is not specified, but it is clear that God's blessing is understood here to extend beyond Israel, and that Israel is in some sense to be the mediator of that. Paul identifies this promise with the gospel, arguing that through the kind of faith that characterized Abraham, the Gentiles, too, can be justified (Gal. 3:8).

The details about Abram's departure for Canaan which are given in vv. 4b–5 were very likely supplied by the later Priestly editor. The more ancient Yahwist narrative has portrayed Abram's response to God's call in the fewest possible number of words: "So Abram went, as the Lord had told him; and Lot went with him" (v. 4a). No superfluous detail distracts from the important point that the Lord has commanded and that Abram has obeyed—without a word, without a question. One is reminded that the various narratives to which this paragraph is an introduction are less about Abraham than they are about Abraham's God, about God's promises, and about God's leading of Abraham (and thus, of Israel) to the fulfillment of those promises. (Lot has to be mentioned here because he will play a role in the subsequent narratives of chapters 13 and 19.)

The first mention of Abram's general destination (apart from the

Priestly editing in v. 5) comes with the report of his arrival in Canaan, where he stops first at Shechem, one of the most ancient and renowned of the Canaanite cities (vv. 5b–6). A "terebinth" (RSV note) was a large, common tree of the area, and the "terebinth of Moreh" seems to have been a renowned cultic site of the Canaanites (see Gen. 35:4; Deut. 11:30; Judg. 9:37). The juxtaposition of the remark of v. 6b, "At that time the Canaanites were in the land," and the notice in v. 7a about the Lord's appearing to Abram is striking. Uprooted from his own land, Abram has come now to a foreign country with its alien cult—but even here his God continues to speak to him. What the Lord now says to Abram is no less surprising, for it takes the form of a second promise: that precisely this land, still ruled by a foreign people and alien gods, shall belong to Abram's descendants. What kind of a promise is this? Into what kind of foolish adventure has the Lord led him? But again, Abram does not complain; and to mark the place, strange as it is, where the Lord has come and spoken to him, he builds an altar (v. 7b).

Shechem, however, is only Abram's first stop in Canaan, for he shortly moves on to the high country farther south, between the Canaanite cities of Bethel and Ai (v. 8). There he builds a second altar, and there he invokes the name of his God ("Yahweh"), thereby affirming his continuing trust in the one who is leading him to a destination still unspecified. Abram's ultimate destination is Hebron, but that is not disclosed until he actually arrives there (see 13:18). For now, the narrative concentrates on the journey itself. Thus, the closing statement of this passage portrays Abram as still on the move, "still going toward the Negeb" (v. 9)—still holding to God's promises (vv. 2–3, 7) and responsive to God's leading (v. 4).

SECOND LESSON: ROMANS 4:1–5, 13–17

To understand these verses, one must understand the argument of the fourth chapter of Romans taken as a whole and the function of that argument within the larger context of Rom. 3:21—8:39.

Beginning in Rom. 3:21 Paul addresses himself to the proposition, presented as early as 1:17 in very summary form, that it is not through devotion to the works of the law that God's righteousness is known, but through faith in Jesus Christ. The point is developed, supported, and illustrated in various ways in chapters 4 and 5, defended against some possible objections in chapters 6 and 7, and then reiterated in chapter 8 as some further points are expounded. The name and example of Abraham are invoked in chapter 4 in order to support the specific contention that, because one is justified "by faith apart from works of law" (3:28), not only the Jews (the circumcised) but also the Gentiles (the uncircumcised) can be justified (3:29–30; the issue raised in v. 31 is not fully examined until 7:7–25). The apostle believes that rather than posing a problem for his argument (as some of Paul's opponents may on occasion have contended), the example of Abraham confirms it, and that is what he sets out to show in chapter 4.

The argument within chapter 4 itself is carefully and clearly developed. The topic to be discussed is introduced in vv. 1–2; the text on which the discussion will be centered is quoted in v. 3; an exposition of the text (drawing upon other texts) follows in vv. 4–22; and the lesson of the text is applied to Christians in vv. 23–25. One important element in the apostle's argument is his observation in vv. 9–12 that Abraham did not receive the commandment to be circumcised (Gen. 17:9–14) until after he had already been reckoned as righteous on the basis of his believing (Gen. 15:6). As for the object and nature of Abraham's faith, no comments are more important than those in vv. 17–21, although our lection officially closes with v. 17. One also needs to take account of Gal. 3:6–18 where, in a somewhat earlier letter, Paul had offered a more specifically christological exegesis of Gen. 15:6 and related texts.

Abraham's status as the father of Israel was well established in Jewish tradition, as various New Testament passages attest (for example, Matt. 3:7–9; John 8:33). Moreover, Jews customarily thought of Abraham in the way he is described in the second-century B.C. *Book of Jubilees*, as "perfect in all his deeds with the Lord, and well-pleasing in righteousness all the days of his life" (23:10, trans. R. H. Charles). Indeed, even within the New Testament one finds Abraham's good deeds cited (to show that faith alone is not enough): "Was not Abraham our father justified by works, when he offered his son Isaac upon the altar?" (James 2:21). Perhaps to counter this kind of argument Paul proposes his own interpretation of Abraham's righteousness, citing not the patriarch's willingness to sacrifice Isaac, but his (and Sarah's) willingness to believe God's promise. The apostle draws his text (Gen. 15:6, cited in v. 3) from the story of God's promising Abraham and Sarah that, despite their advanced age and Sarah's barrenness, a son would be born to them, and that their descendants would be as innumerable as the stars in the heavens.

From Paul's comments in v. 4, it is apparent that he regards the verbs "believed" and "was reckoned" as the two key words of the text. Believing is contrasted with working, and having something reckoned to one ("as a gift," v. 4) is contrasted with receiving one's due wages. The apostle's point is that, contrary to common Jewish belief, Abraham's righteousness was not something he had earned by reason of his good deeds, but something that had been bestowed upon him quite apart from his deserving it, solely on the basis of his believing. This point is both generalized and radicalized in v. 5, where the verb translated as "trusts"(RSV) could just as readily be rendered "believes." The declaration here that God "justifies the ungodly" anticipates the one in 5:6 that "Christ died for the ungodly," that is, for "the undeserving," those who do not presume that good deeds have entitled them to something from God.

The contrast between faith and works is more specifically articulated in vv. 13–15 where, as in 3:21, 28, the apostle writes of the law's inability to bring righteousness (vv. 13, 14). Indeed, he even goes so far as to suggest a link between the law and sin (v. 15). This is one of several places in the early chapters of Romans where the complex issue of the status and function of the law begins to emerge (see also 3:20, 31; 5:13–14, 20–21), but there is no full discussion of it until 7:7–25. For the argument of chapter 4 itself, therefore, vv. 16–17, to which one should add vv. 18–21, are more important.

Verses 16–21 allow us to understand more precisely what Paul sees in Abraham's faith that prompts him to commend it as exemplary. First, the object of Abraham's faith is "the God . . . who gives life to the dead and calls into existence the things that do not exist" (v. 17). The creation and the redemption of life are both in view here. For Abraham and Sarah, the birth of a son would be the bringing of life from bodies "as good as dead" (v. 19), something no less awesome than the wonder of creation itself. Second, the "hope" that is involved in Abraham's believing is contrasted with the ordinary hopes by

which human beings generally live: "In hope he believed against
hope . . ." (v. 18). That is, contrary to what one would normally regard
as a realistic hope—given the human condition of this aged couple—
Abraham was sustained in his believing by a hope in the reality of God's
promises. Finally, then, the patriarch's "believing" is characterized by
his unwavering trust in God's power to bestow the life that had been
promised, and his giving "glory" to God (vv. 20–21).

We may conclude that for Paul, faith means (a) giving up the vain
attempt to create or to restore life out of one's own meager, human
resources (compare Rom. 1:21); and (b) acknowledging with gratitude
one's absolute dependence upon the promise and power of God.

GOSPEL: JOHN 4:5–26 (27–30, 39–42)

A long and complex compositional history probably lies behind our
canonical Gospel of John, although scholars are not agreed on exactly
what that was or how it developed. It is clear, nonetheless, that the
theme of Jesus' self-revelation pervades this Gospel and gives to the
whole a basic theological integrity. Moreover, even though several
different sets of editorial fingerprints have been discerned in the
Gospel as we have it, the Gospel also continues to exhibit a certain
dramatic integrity, both in its overall structure and within its individual narratives. This story of Jesus' encounter with the Samaritan
woman at Jacob's well has integrity of both sorts, so to deal with any
one part of it will require the interpreter to take account of the
narrative in its entirety—including not only vv. 27–30 and 39–42,
which the lectionary places within a parenthesis, but also vv. 31–38.

The drama begins even as the scene is set in vv. 5–9: Jesus, a Jew
among Samaritans—whom Jews traditionally considered as little better than Gentiles—seeks relief from the midday heat by stopping to
rest at Jacob's well. There is no reflection here on how God's Son
could have been "wearied . . . with his journey" (v. 6), or why he must
ask a woman to draw water for him (v. 7). These introductory verses
emphasize only how strange it is that any Jewish man would make
such a request of a Samaritan woman (v. 9; cf. v. 27). The narrative
proper may be divided into two parts: (1) Jesus' conversation with the
woman (vv. 10–26); and (2) the woman's return to the city to tell of it
(vv. 27–42). The conversation between Jesus and his disciples that

stands within the second part of the narrative (vv. 31–38) helps to emphasize one of the main points of the story. It also interjects an element of dramatic suspense, because an explanation of why the Samaritans are coming out to Jesus (v. 30) is thereby delayed until v. 39.

Here, as in every Johannine narrative, the central figure is Jesus, so one should really speak not of *his* encounter with the Samaritan woman, but of *her* encounter with him. And here, as throughout this Gospel, Jesus is presented as the one through whom eternal life is given—now—to those who have eyes to see and hearts to believe that he is the Christ. The setting of this conversation at Jacob's well allows the narrator to describe the life that Jesus brings as "living water" (vv. 10, 14), which accords with other important Johannine images such as "bread" (6:35, 51; etc.), "way" (14:6), and "vine" (15:1–8). It recurs in 7:38 (where it is associated specifically with the Spirit, 7:39) when Jesus says, "If any one thirst, let him come to me and drink"; and this, in a sense, is what one sees at the end of the present narrative when the Samaritans are shown coming to Jesus (4:30, 40).

One fascinating aspect of this story is the portrayal of how the Samaritan woman gradually comes to faith during the course of her conversation with Jesus. Initially, she cannot receive his promise of life because she is thinking only of strictly physical needs and possibilities (vv. 11–12). After Jesus' elaboration of his promise (vv. 13–14) she begins to perceive that something more is involved (v. 15), but there is still no true understanding.

The first significant breakthrough comes when Jesus calls her to account for her disreputable conduct (vv. 16–18), from which she concludes that this man must be "a prophet" (v. 19). Her subsequent question about the true place of worship (v. 20) raises an issue on which Jews and Samaritans differed, and it certainly would have been regarded as the proper religious question to ask. One wonders, however, whether she poses it only to try to divert attention from her own situation—a tactic rather like that of the embarrassed airline passenger who has just discovered that the person in the next seat is a member of the clergy! Whatever her motive, Jesus takes the question seriously, even though he chooses neither of the traditional religious options to which she has referred. Declaring that true worship is not to be identified with any particular sanctuary (v. 21), he focuses rather

upon the worshipers themselves (v. 23–24), suggesting that the authen-
ticity of their worship depends upon their relationship to God. The
references here to God as "Father" are important (vv. 21, 23), for
Jesus knows God as his Father in a special sense, and those who
believe in Jesus are to accept his Father as their Father, too (see
20:17b). Only those who acknowledge that they are God's "children"
can "worship the Father in spirit and truth" (v. 23; see 1:12–13;
3:5–6).

The moment would seem to call for an affirmation of Jesus as
Messiah (Christ) and as the Son in whom the fullness of the Father's
gift of life is already present. But the Samaritan woman has not heard
Jesus say that the coming hour (v. 21) *now is* (v. 23), and she can still
only affirm the traditional teaching about a future Messiah (v. 25). It is
left to Jesus, in the climactic pronouncement of the whole conversation, to identity himself with that Messiah: "I who speak to you am
he" (v. 26—a characteristically Johannine "I am" saying). Finally,
the woman begins to reckon with the reality of the life in whose
presence she stands, and she becomes at least a tentative evangelist of
the good news of the Messiah's arrival (see vv. 28–29).

The portrayal of this woman's dawning consciousness of who Jesus
is does not constitute the whole story, however. This is also a story
about the universalism of Jesus' messiahship and mission. To the
Samaritans as well as to the Jews he has disclosed himself as the one
who bears the gift of eternal life. The only unambiguous "confession
of faith" that one hears in this narrative, and the one with which it
concludes, is not uttered by the woman, but by the Samaritan citizens
when they declare that Jesus "is indeed the Savior of the world"
(v. 42). While the despised Samaritans are not actually Gentiles, Jesus'
presence among them and their response to him clearly anticipate the
encounter Philip will have with "some Greeks" in Jerusalem (12:20–
22). In this Gospel Jesus is often presented as the "Savior of the
world," even if the title occurs only here (see, e.g., 3:16–17; 6:33;
12:32, 47). Jesus' conversation with his disciples (vv. 31–38) is related
to the missionary theme in this passage. It is significant that the
conversation takes place while the news about Jesus is being spread
abroad in the Samaritan city, and that it concerns both the mission of
Jesus (v. 34) and that of his disciples (v. 38).

Finally, one should notice the distinction that is drawn here between believing in Jesus "because of the woman's testimony" (v. 39) and believing in him "because of his word" (v. 41). The woman's role in spreading the word of the Messiah's arrival is not disparaged, but neither is it emphasized. It prompts at least a preliminary kind of faith, but one that is still secondhand. The Samaritans themselves recognize this when they say to the woman, "It is no longer because of your words that we believe, for we have heard for ourselves . . ." (v. 42). Here, as in the following narrative about the healing of an official's son (4:46–54), it is above all Jesus' own life-bringing word to which faith is a response and by which faith is nourished (cf. 4:41–42 with 4:50, 53).

The Third Sunday in Lent

Lutheran	Roman Catholic	Episcopal	Pres/UCC/Chr	Meth/COCU
Isa. 42:14–21	Exod. 17:3–7	Exod. 17:1–7	Exod. 24:12–18	Exod. 17:3–7
Eph. 5:8–14	Rom. 5:1–2, 5–8	Rom. 5:1–11	Rom. 5:1–5	Rom. 5:1–11
John 9:1–41 or John 9:13–17, 34–39	John 4:5–42 or John 4:5–15, 19–26, 39, 40–42	John 4:5–26 (27–38) 39–42	John 4:5–15, 19–26	John 4:5–42

Sight is regarded by most people as their most precious sensory faculty, and blindness is generally more feared than the loss of hearing, or even of a limb. This accounts for the frequency with which languages make use of sight metaphors and for their extraordinary power to communicate. Two of the lections for this Sunday employ such metaphors, and the closely related symbolism of light and darkness occurs in the third. We must pay careful attention, however, to the various ways in which the texts employ this imagery.

FIRST LESSON: ISAIAH 42:14–21

The anonymous prophet to whom the oracles of Isaiah 40—55 are attributed is generally identified as "Second Isaiah" in order to distinguish him from Isaiah of Jerusalem, from whom most of the prophetic oracles in chapters 1–39 derive. Second Isaiah was active during the period of Israel's exile in Babylon, between the destruction of Jerusalem in 587 B.C. and the fall of the Babylonian empire in 539. The words of comfort and hope with which the collection of his oracles opens in chapter 40 (vv. 1–2) are representative of this prophet's emphasis: Israel will be delivered from her oppressors and returned to her own land, for her disobedience has been sufficiently punished, and God will turn in mercy to pardon and vindicate her.

Our lection falls into two distinct sections, and even though the "blind" are mentioned in each, the metaphor is used rather differently in the two cases. Verses 14–17 are usually regarded as constituting a single, relatively self-contained unit, whereas vv. 18–21 are only the opening lines of a passage that must be regarded as extending through v. 25.

In vv. 14–17 the speaker is God, and the oracle opens (v. 14a) with an allusion to the traditional Hebrew lament "How long, O Lord?" (especially frequent in the Psalms—for example, Pss. 13:1–2; 35:17; 74:10; 79:5; but also found elsewhere—for example, Isa. 6:11; Hab. 1:2). As if in response to this kind of plaintive cry, Israel is assured that, after a "long time" of apparent indifference to her petitions, God is about to intervene in her behalf. The striking image of the Lord as a woman in labor (v. 14b) may be intended to emphasize God's protracted agonizing over his people's distress. Finally, however, deliverance will come, and that is described in vv. 15–16. The transformation of nature portrayed in v. 15 could be taken as an allusion to the Lord's "way" through the land, and thus as an affirmation of God's power to intervene in the natural course of things, changing what is otherwise unchangeable (see 40:3–5). More probably, however, the thought is of God's judgment (see, for example, Ps. 107:33–34), in which case Israel's oppressors, her Babylonian captors, would be in view, as they also are in v. 17.

Israel's own destiny is the subject of v. 16, which is the heart of this particular oracle. Here the "blind" are those who languish in exile, unable to see any "light at the end of the tunnel" of their present captivity. It is not Israel's disobedience or apostasy that is being depicted (as, for example, in Isa. 59:9–10), but the exiles' sense of

hopelessness and of helplessness—their sense of having been abandoned by God. These "blind" are assured that they have not been
forsaken, and that their God will lead them out of the darkness of their
exile and return them safely to their own land. No translation can do
full justice to the prophet's formulation of God's promise, "These are
the things I will do," because the Hebrew term rendered here as
"things" could also be translated as "words." As in 55:10–11 (the
most important passage for understanding this prophet's conception
of God's "word"), the thought embraces both what God purposes and
what God accomplishes—indeed, the whole of God's creative and
redemptive activity. Because "the word of our God will stand for
ever" (40:8), the exiles need not despair.

Verses 18–21 are drawn from an oracle that runs through v. 25. This
is entirely distinct from the oracle of vv. 14–17, even though here, too,
the imagery of blindness/sight is effectively employed (vv. 18–20). It
would appear that the exiles in their despair have charged God with
being deaf to their cries and blind to their needs, because in vv. 18–19
the Lord calls upon Israel to consider who really are the "deaf" and
the "blind." It is not God, but God's "servant" Israel, who is the
blind one (v. 19)! In the context of this oracle, deafness and blindness
symbolize Israel's lack of understanding, her inability to discern
God's ways and God's purposes even in her own history (v. 20).

The intention of this oracle, however, is not to condemn Israel for
her lack of insight; blindness, it has been noted, is an affliction, not a
sin! Rather, it is to call Israel to "hear" and to "see" what she has so
far been unable to accept, that even her present experiences of suffering and of exile lie within the sphere of God's purpose (vv. 22–24).
These the prophet understands to be God's judgment upon the
people's past disobedience: "Who gave up Jacob to the spoiler, and
Israel to the robbers? Was it not the Lord, against whom we have
sinned? . . ." (v. 24a). It is because Israel has not yet realized this
(v. 25) that Second Isaiah is calling the exiles to consider the meaning
of their present circumstances. He is also calling them, however, to
consider what the future holds (v. 23).

Two points in these oracles deserve particular notice. In the oracle
of vv. 18–25, the rhetorical question posed in v. 23 is of special
interest: "Who among you will give ear to this, will attend and listen

for the time to come?'' If the exiles will accept their suffering as lying within God's purpose, then they will find release from that suffering and perceive what lies beyond it. From the Servant Songs of 42:1–4; 49:1–6; 50:4–11; and 52:13—53:12 it is clear that Second Isaiah views Israel's suffering as an integral part of her mission to be ''a light to the nations'' for justice and for salvation. What lies beyond the suffering is indicated in the following oracle (43:1–7): the exiles will (soon) be delivered from their captivity and returned home. Meanwhile, however, it is not to her misery but to her mission that Israel should attend, because it is not for slavery in Babylon but for the service of God that she has been set apart.

In the oracle of vv. 14–17, the principal affirmation is not that the exiles, so far helplessly ''blind'' to any hope for deliverance, will be given their sight. It is, rather, that God is present with them in their darkness to guide them along paths that they could not otherwise traverse: ''And I will lead the blind in a way that they know not, in paths that they have not known I will guide them'' (v. 16). The prophet's good news for the exiles is that God has not abandoned them, and that they do not have to find their own way through the darkness of their present circumstances. This can also be good news for us, for we have all experienced what it means to be exiled in helplessness and alienated from hope. It is important to recognize, however, that our text is addressed to the situation of a *community* in exile and without hope. Therefore, when it assures us that God is present, leading us through the darkness and into the light, it is also summoning us to accept and affirm one another as God's people—and to be present for one another even as God is present for us.

SECOND LESSON: EPHESIANS 5:8–14

The author of Ephesians (probably not Paul himself, but someone writing several decades after the apostle's death) thinks of his readers as gentile Christians who, before their conversion, were ''darkened in their understanding, alienated from the life of God . . . '' (4:18), and corrupted ''through deceitful lusts'' (4:22). In 4:1—6:20, the section from which our lection has been drawn, the author is reminding his readers that their conversion should have changed all of that (see 4:1, 20–21). His fundamental appeal is well expressed in 4:22–24: ''Put off your old nature which belongs to your former manner of life . . . , and put on the new nature, created after the likeness of God in true righteousness and holiness.''

The immediate context of our lection is the pericope that runs from 5:3 to 5:20. Within this, vv. 8–14 constitute an identifiable subunit, characterized by the use of the metaphor of ''light'' to describe the believer's new life (vv. 8, 9, 13, 14; compare vv. 11–12). Thus, contrary to the punctuation adopted in the RSV, one should regard v. 8 as the beginning of a new sentence (correctly, NEB, JB, etc.); v. 7 does not introduce what follows but concludes what precedes. In vv. 8–14 as throughout Ephesians, one finds many ideas and expressions that had already become a fixed part of the church's tradition, from which this author has freely borrowed in order to remind his readers of that to which they have been committed since their conversion.

One striking thing about this passage is the way the author employs the metaphor of darkness and light in order to draw a contrast between who his readers ''once'' were and who they ''now'' are (v. 8a). He does not say that once they were ''*in* the darkness,'' but are now ''*in* the light.'' Rather, he says that once they ''*were* darkness,'' but now they ''*are* light in the Lord.'' They had not just been overcome by darkness; they had actually *become* darkness. Their conversion does not just mean ''seeing the light,'' but actually *becoming* light. We should pay close attention to what this suggests about the nature of sin and of salvation. This text does not allow us to think of ourselves as having been only the victims of sin; it requires that we face up to the fact that we have served as sin's agents. Similarly, it does not allow us to think of ourselves as only beneficiaries of God's grace, but proposes that ''in the Lord'' we have actually become bearers of it. The text evokes an image of people who have not only been illumined by the light of the gospel, but who have been so deeply touched and transformed by it that they themselves have become incandescent—''the light of the world'' (Matt. 5:14).

In vv. 8–14 as well as in Ephesians overall, one meets the typically Pauline pattern of indicatives followed by imperatives. The indicative in 5:8a leads to the imperatives in vv. 8b, 10, and 11, just as the indicatives in 4:1–16 and 5:1–2 have led to the imperatives in 4:17–32 and 5:3—6:20, respectively—and just as, on a larger scale, the affirmations that predominate in chapters 1–3 have led to the appeals that predominate in chapters 4–6. Why is this so? It is certainly not because the writer doubts the reality of the new, "luminescent" life that a believer is given "in the Lord." Rather, precisely because the gift of new life inheres in one's relationship to the Lord, that gift is inseparable from the giver, and believers are always accountable to him for what they have received (see, for example, 4:1–6).

In the words of Col. 1:12–13, with which our author was probably acquainted, believers have been "delivered . . . from the dominion of darkness" and "transferred [into] the kingdom of his beloved Son," where they "share in the inheritance of the saints in light." To be "light" rather than "darkness" is to be bound to a new Lord, and those who are now "light" rather than "darkness" should conduct themselves as "children of light" (Eph. 5:8b), radiating goodness, righteousness, and truth in their lives (v. 9). Some examples of "the unfruitful works of darkness" mentioned in v. 11 may be seen in vv. 3–4, but it is not entirely clear how one is to "expose" these— especially because of the warning in v. 12 not even "to speak" about them (compare v. 3). The idea may be that no words are needed, since the luminescent behavior of the "children of light" will cast the powerful searchlight of God's own judgment upon them (see v. 13).

The appeal to "try to learn what is pleasing to the Lord" (v. 10) deserves special attention. The RSV translation, "try to learn," is a good rendering of a word Paul himself has employed in Rom. 12:2 and Phil. 1:10 (where respectively the RSV translations "prove" and "approve" are much less satisfactory). Neither Paul nor the author of Ephesians presumes that "what is pleasing to the Lord" has been spelled out anywhere in detail—not in Scripture, or even in the teachings of Jesus; and neither of them presumes to offer his own detailed ethical prescriptions. Instead, they urge believers to apply themselves to the task of discerning, within the particular circumstances of their own time and place, what is required of those who are recipients of the gracious love of God bestowed in Christ (in Ephesians, see 4:32; 5:2; cf. 5:25, 29).

Our lection concludes in v. 14 with a quotation, drawn either from the church's baptismal liturgy or from a baptismal hymn:

> Awake, O sleeper, and arise from the dead,
> and Christ shall give you light.

In a baptismal context these words constitute a call to nonbelievers to commit themselves to Christ, and thus to receive the new life God offers in Christ (see 2:1, 5). Addressed to those who have already been initiated into the community of faith through baptism, as they are in Ephesians and when they are read in any congregation, they are a summons to renew that commitment and to reaffirm one's new life in Christ. In either case, it is important to notice that the appeal is based on a promise, not on a threat. Authentically Christian preaching never attempts to shame or to frighten people into commitment and renewal; that would not be genuinely *gospel,* "good news." Rather, it invites them to accept the reality of God's grace and forgiveness, and in receiving that to be delivered from death to life, from darkness to light.

GOSPEL: JOHN 9:1–41

Although this narrative as it stands is thoroughly Johannine in style and point of view, it is probable that the evangelist has developed it on the basis of the traditional healing account which is still visible in vv. 1–7 (cf. Mark 10:46–52, with parallels; and especially Mark 8:22–26). The remainder of the chapter seems to represent a dramatic expansion of that, and can be readily divided into several distinct scenes: vv. 8–12, 13–17, 18–23, 24–34, and 35–41. If only part of the chapter is employed as a lection, the integrity of each of these scenes should be respected when choosing the verses to be read; and the integrity of the narrative as a whole should be respected, even if just one of these scenes is being examined.

Viewed with reference to its most general theological function, the purpose of this narrative is to present Jesus as the one who brings light into a world that is, like the blind beggar, groping about in darkness. It may thus be read as a narrative restatement of the proclamation in the Gospel's prologue, "The true light that enlightens every man was coming into the world" (1:9). More immediately, however, it serves as a dramatization of Jesus' announcement in 8:12, "I am the light of the world; he who follows me will not walk in darkness, but will have the light of life." Here "light" symbolizes (true) life, and "darkness" is a symbol of (spiritual) death. We are in touch with a theme that pervades the whole of this Gospel: Jesus, God's Son, has been sent by his Father in order that the world might "believe," and that in its "believing . . . might have life in his name" (20:31).

These Johannine interests are evident from the very beginning of the chapter, in the healing narrative itself (vv. 1–7). The real focus here, due probably to the evangelist's reworking of his source, is on the words of Jesus in vv. 3–5. One should observe, first, that what is about to take place is presented as a witness to "the works of God" (v. 3; cf. 11:4). This does not mean, however, that the evangelist intends it to be read only as a story about Jesus' service to the indigent and the infirm. Rather, as the comment in v. 4 suggests, he intends that it should be read as another of the "signs" (see v. 16)—like those performed in Galilee (2:1–11 and 4:46–54)—that Jesus has been "sent" by his Father to bring the light of life into the world.

Second, one should not miss the clearly deliberate use of the first person plural in v. 4: "*We* must work the works of the one who sent me. . . . " Jesus' disciples, to whom these words are addressed, are also to be doing God's work of bringing life to the world—a task for which they will be commissioned shortly before Jesus' death (see chap. 17, especially v. 18). Moreover, they need to realize that their time for this, like Jesus' time, is limited: "Night comes, when no one can work." One needs to realize that, lacking electricity, neither night shifts nor night life could be taken for granted in the ancient world (see also 11:9–10), and that Jesus is about to break the law by kneading clay on the Sabbath (see v. 14). Clearly, for this evangelist, "being religious" sometimes conflicts with doing "the works of God," and when that happens, God's works must take priority!

However, the most important thing to notice here is the pronouncement of v. 5, which not only echoes the "I am" saying of 8:12 but, by introducing the healing itself, signals the main point of this whole passage: "As long as I am in the world, I am the light of the world." With these words, Jesus mixes a muddy salve and applies it to the beggar's unseeing eyes (v. 6), for this blind man represents the world, locked in the darkness of death and needing that light apart from which no meaningful life is possible. Following Jesus' instructions, the beggar washes his eyes in the pool of Siloam, and comes back seeing (v. 7). The name of the pool, we are told, means "sent," and the evangelist surely wants us to think of Jesus, whom he frequently portrays as one "sent" from God; see, for example, 5:36, 38; 6:29, 57; 7:29; 8:42; 10:36—and many other instances, including those in which a different Greek word is used, as in 9:4. We are to recognize that the power to restore the man's sight resided neither in the salve that was applied to his eyes nor in the water that washed it off. It resided in Jesus' presence, and in Jesus' reaching out into the blind man's darkness with light and life. (This imagery reappears in 12:35–36, 46.)

The five subsequent episodes may be examined from at least three different angles. First, we may read them for what they tell us about the original readers of this Gospel, because one major issue confronting them seems to be reflected here. The beggar, as various interpreters have suggested, probably represents those Jews of the evangelist's day who, because of their open belief in Jesus, had been excommunicated from the synagogue (see vv. 22, 34, and 16:2–4). An important function of this story would have been to encourage others to do the same. Thus, read as a story about the evangelist's church, it is a story about the way faith requires a willingness to make a radical break with one's past, and even to risk the hostility of others (see 12:42–43).

It is possible, in the second place, to read this as a story about the Pharisees, who are also identified here simply as ''the Jews'' (vv. 18, 22). In this Gospel, ''the Jews'' symbolize persisting unbelief and opposition to the truth. In their interrogation of the beggar (vv. 13–17), their question about *how* he has been given his sight soon changes to a question about *who* it is who has accomplished this. That something marvelous has occurred they do not doubt, but while some incline to interpret the healing as evidence that Jesus has come from God, others argue that his violation of the Sabbath proves him to be a sinner. Here as elsewhere it is apparent that for this evangelist Jesus' signs provide only an ambiguous witness; while they may lead some to faith, they cause others to be hardened in their unbelief (see especially the assessment of signs in 12:37–43).

During his second interrogation by the Pharisees (vv. 24–34), the beggar teasingly asks them whether they, too, are interested in becoming disciples of Jesus. No answer is required, of course, because it is clear that the Pharisees have no sense of needing anything that Jesus has to offer. This is brought out in the very last scene (vv. 35–41). In response to the beggar's confession of faith, Jesus speaks of his having come into the world for judgment, ''that those who do not see may see, and that those who see may become blind.'' When some Pharisees who have overheard this ask, "Surely you don't mean that we are blind, too?" (TEV), Jesus replies, "If you were blind, you would have no guilt; but now that you say, 'We see,' your guilt remains."

A comparison with the words of 3:19–21 helps to clarify the point: Jesus' coming into the world means sight (life) for those who recognize that they are blind, and who come to the light of his presence. But Jesus' coming means judgment for those who, thinking that they "see" when they do not, refuse to come to the light, and so become blind indeed. As a story about the Pharisees, this is a story about all of us—specifically, about our pious presumption that we already "see" and therefore do not need to come to the light of God's presence.

Third, this can be read as a story about the beggar. When acquaintances ask him how he has gained his sight, he can only reply that the successful remedy was concocted by a man named Jesus, of whose present whereabouts he knows nothing (vv. 8–12). Just as it was not faith that had brought him his sight, so the cure has not brought him to faith! Later, asked by the Pharisees to help them decide whether Jesus is "from God" (vv. 13–17), the beggar can still say only, "He is a prophet"—that is, a person endowed with special religious insight (cf. 4:19). Subsequently, after the Pharisees have decided that Jesus is a sinner, the beggar is forced to think more deeply about the matter, and finally lines himself up on the side of Jesus, saying, "If this man were not from God, he could do nothing" (vv. 24–34).

It is only in the last scene, however, when Jesus reappears and discloses himself as the Son of man, that this beggar actually makes a confession of faith: "Lord, I believe" (vv. 35–41). The evangelist wants us to understand that the decisive revelation was not given in the miracle of the man's healing, but in the reality of Jesus' "having found him" (v. 35), being present with him, and addressing him (see v. 37: "You have seen him, and it is he who speaks to you").

Finally, then, the beggar's story is a story about Jesus, the light of the world, who, penetrating the world's darkness, opens the eyes of humanity to God and bestows true life. Viewing this Gospel overall (as one must always do), it is clear that Jesus is the light of the world because in him God's love for the world is present and active (see 3:16; 13:1; etc.). Love penetrates the darkness and provides the illumination for true life; and to "believe" in Jesus as the light of the world and commit oneself to "walking" in that light (see 12:35–36) means accepting from him the badge of discipleship: the "new commandment" to love one another (13:34–35).

The Fourth Sunday in Lent

Lutheran	Roman Catholic	Episcopal	Pres/UCC/Chr	Meth/COCU
Hos. 5:15—6:2	1 Sam. 16:1b, 6–7, 10–13a	1 Sam. 16:1–13	2 Sam. 5:1–5	1 Sam. 16:1–18
Rom. 8:1–10	Eph. 5:8–14	Eph. 5:(1–7) 8–14	Eph. 5:8–14	Eph. 5:8–14
Matt. 20:17–28	John 9:1–41 or John 9:1, 6–9, 13–17, 34–38	John 9:1–13 (14–27) 28–38	John 9:1–11	John 9:1–41

Apart from the obvious but not entirely significant fact that a "third day" is mentioned both in the First Lesson and in the Gospel, nothing in particular binds any one of the three texts appointed for reading on this Sunday to either one of the others. They are, one may say, really three distinct lessons and are best approached as such.

FIRST LESSON: HOSEA 5:15—6:2

By inserting the word "saying" between 5:15 and 6:1, the RSV gives the impression that the two verses are certainly to be connected. In fact, no such linking word occurs in the Hebrew text, and 5:15 is more closely related to 5:8–14 than to what follows in chapter 6 (see NEB and TEV). Therefore, the first verse of our lection needs to be examined in the light of the seven preceding verses, for vv. 8–15 constitute one distinct prophetic oracle. Moreover, along with 6:1–2 we need to consider 6:3, for these three verses certainly stand together. While breaking off this lection with v. 2 gives prominence to the "third day" reference (thereby suggesting a connection with the Gospel lection), it only obscures the point of the oracle itself—to which the "third day" reference is quite incidental. Indeed, a case can be made for including also 6:4–6 within this lection (see below).

The historical background of the oracle that stands before us in 5:8–15 is the international crisis of 738–732 B.C. Israel (the northern kingdom is referred to here as "Ephraim") and Syria, allied in an attempt to withstand the Assyrians, tried unsuccessfully to replace Judah's king (Ahaz) in order to have the support of the southern kingdom for their cause. In this oracle, Hosea (a northern prophet) anticipates that the present enmity between the northern and southern kingdoms will mean the ultimate ruin of both, and he interprets that as God's judgment upon them for trusting in international, military alliances rather than in the God to whom they are bound by sacred covenant. When in 5:13 God's judgment is likened to an incurable disease or sore, a wasting from within the body itself, Hosea may have in mind the moral corruption that can eat away at a body politic and contribute to its ultimate ruin. Similarly, when God's judgment is portrayed in v. 14 as a ravaging lion, tearing his victim apart and carrying it off piece by piece, the prophet may be thinking of predators like the Assyrians, for whom Ephraim and Judah—already weakened by their own folly—were becoming ever easier prey.

Perhaps we are to think of a lion leaving a carcass and withdrawing to his den when, in v. 15, we hear the Lord say, "I will return again to my place. . . . " But even if the imagery of v. 14 is not continued, the idea of an absent God that is conveyed here is striking enough in itself. God's absence is understood here not as a further punishment but as an act of grace. Its purpose is to allow God's people an opportunity to contemplate the reason why they stand under judgment, to acknowledge their guilt, and to repent. Who has not experienced a sense of God's withdrawing, of God's absence? This text allows us, first, to acknowledge the reality of such experiences. Second, and even more important, it suggests that God's being absent from us is but a special mode of God's being present with us—for it makes little sense to speak of the "absence" of someone whose presence we have never experienced or cannot anticipate. Hosea's portrayal of an absent God is, in its own way, a part of the prophet's testimony to the continuing reality of God's presence and faithfulness, another way of bearing witness to a loving and caring God.

The next verses (6:1–3) read more like a traditional penitential song than like one of Hosea's own prophetic oracles. Whether sung by pilgrims to Jerusalem or by the temple priests on behalf of the people, perhaps in a time of national crisis, the song expresses confidence that the Lord who has inflicted punishment will now bind up the people's wounds, and that they will again be able to experience the Lord's presence (see "live before him," v. 2; "know the Lord," v. 3). This conception of God as the one who heals and forgives, and by whom life is sustained, is absolutely fundamental to Israel's faith and to the whole Judeo-Christian tradition.

The confidence that God will sustain Israel's life as a people is expressed in v. 2 as a hope that "after two days [the Lord] will revive us; on the third day he will raise us up. . . . " A Christian reader will inevitably think of Jesus' resurrection "on the third day." In fact, however, the image here is not of resurrection from the dead but of getting up out of a sickbed, as in Psalm 41 (see especially vv. 3 and 10), and the restoration to health of a whole people is in mind. "After two days . . . on the third day" means simply "in a short while."

Is the penitential song of 6:1–3 an adequate response to the hope expressed in 5:15 that Israel will acknowledge her guilt and seek the face of her God? Some interpreters believe that the prophet has quoted these words of the liturgy in order to criticize them, not because he wants to commend them. If so, the criticism would come in 6:4–6 where Israel's love (of God) is likened to "a morning cloud" and to "the dew that goes early away" (v. 4), and where the Lord says, "I desire steadfast love and not sacrifice, the knowledge of God rather than burnt offerings" (v. 6). But even if the penitential song of 6:1–3 is not being criticized, one does well to keep the words of the following verses in view. According to Hosea, the penitence to which God's people are called must find expression, finally, in their "steadfast love"—that is, in their renewed and constant obedience to the one with whom they are bound by covenant, and in whose gracious presence they have their life.

SECOND LESSON: ROMANS 8:1–10

The chapter from which this lesson has been drawn develops the thesis, offered in Rom. 7:6, that "we are discharged from the law, dead to that which held us captive, so that we serve not under the old written code but in the new life of the Spirit." Life "under the old written code" (the law) is described in 7:7–25. Beginning in 8:1 Paul turns to a discussion of "the new life of the Spirit." Strictly speaking, our lection should include v. 11 because, as all of the major translations recognize, it follows closely on vv. 9–10.

Our lection opens with a gloriously liberating affirmation: "The law of the Spirit of life in Christ Jesus" frees believers from "the law of sin and death" by which they are otherwise condemned (vv. 1–2). However, one must be very clear not to misunderstand what Paul means here by freedom. He is certainly not thinking of liberation from the responsibility to understand and do God's will; later in the letter he will charge the Roman Christians to give themselves over to this without reservation (12:1–2). Nor is he thinking about liberation from the frustration that one may feel at being unable to know and do God's will perfectly, in spite of one's best efforts; he himself experiences such frustration (see, e.g., Phil. 1:21–24). This text is also misunderstood if one supposes that "no condemnation for those who are in Christ Jesus" means that believers are not subject to the judgment of God; again, later in this same letter the apostle will declare that "we shall all stand before the judgment seat of God" where each "shall give account of himself to God" (14:10–12).

What, then, does liberation mean in this context? Paul believes that sin and (its consequence) death are able to exert their power through the law (thus, "the law of sin and death," v. 2). Therefore, to be liberated from the law means to be delivered, not from "sinning" or "dying," but from a life spiritually tyrannized and therefore morally paralyzed by the threat of sin and death. A less theological and more existential statement of this occurs in Romans 6, where the apostle associates baptism into Christ with the "crucifixion" of one's "old self" (see vv. 3–4, 6–7). The old self is intent on self-commendation and the attainment of position (see 2 Cor. 5:12); but those who have died with Christ "live no longer for themselves but for him who for their sake died and was raised" (2 Cor. 5:15).

Therefore, deliverance from sin and death means liberation from the fatuous presumption that by our own planning and achieving "life can be beautiful," meaningful, and fulfilled. It means release from the delusion, of which clever advertisers have long since learned to take advantage, that if we can somehow look "right," smell "right," cultivate the "right" habits and acquire the "right" things, we will also *be* "right"! But Paul declares that believers are freed from this fantasy that "right[eous]ness" can be attained on the basis of their own resources.

Our text speaks of more than just liberation, however. It also speaks, in its own way, of commitment. Liberation in the Pauline sense involves not only freedom *from,* but always also freedom *for.* This conviction is one of the elements involved in the contrast, drawn in v. 4 and then elaborated in vv. 5–8, between "walking according to the flesh" and "walking according to the Spirit." To what do these metaphors refer?

In this as in many other passages, Paul uses the word "flesh" to include much more than just the physical appetites. Here it refers to the whole person as she or he continues to be ruled by the "old self" and its delusions. Therefore, to "walk according to the flesh" means to try to orient oneself on life's path by means of a compass whose needle never swings true. The parallel expressions in 1 Cor. 3:3 (to walk "like ordinary men"—oriented to merely human wisdom and standards) and 2 Cor. 5:7 (to walk "by sight"—according only to the appearance of things) are helpful. Paul is thinking of those who are committed to standards of judgment that are finally inappropriate to their status as children of God and members of the human community. Because "walking according to the flesh" is fundamentally a matter of *who* and *whose* one understands oneself to *be,* Paul can say that "the mind that is set on the flesh is hostile to God" (v. 7). By way of contrast, those who "walk according to the Spirit" are committed to "the things of the Spirit" (v. 5). What are these? Not just prayer and meditation. Paul means, inclusively, whatever is appropriate to one's status as a child of God, so he can write elsewhere of walking in a way that accords with God's call (1 Cor. 7:17; 1 Thess. 2:12) and according to faith (2 Cor. 5:7). This is also a walking "in newness of life" (Rom. 6:4), because in Christ one's "old self" has died, along with its fantasies and false standards. What takes its place is a whole "new creation" (2 Cor. 5:17), the essence of which is the rule of Christ's love (2 Cor. 5:14). This love is "the power of God" which, paradoxically, he understands to have been revealed decisively in the apparent weakness of the cross (see 1 Cor. 1:18–25).

Because Paul, in keeping with the whole biblical tradition, thinks of the Spirit primarily in terms of power, the Spirit, too, is associated with love (Rom. 5:5; Gal. 5:22). Walking "according to the Spirit" means, then, to live in accord with the standard of love disclosed and established in the cross. It means to allow oneself not only to be renewed by that love, but also to be empowered, guided, and finally judged by it. It means to be *for others* as God, in Christ, is "for us" (see Rom. 8:31). Thus, Paul warns the Romans that if they injure the brother (or sister) for whom Christ has (also) died, they are "no longer walking in love" (Rom. 14:15). It is clear, then, that the believer's freedom *from* the tyranny of self-will and self-seeking also involves a new freedom *for* others. Even as God's love—in Christ—liberates us from the shackles of sin and death, it also binds us to one another —in Christ—for a mutual upbuilding in love.

In vv. 3-4, probably drawing on traditional creedal formulations, Paul identifies the means by which believers are granted this new freedom and called to this new commitment. Since the law is powerless to save (because it allows us to suppose that by our own moral achievements we can be righteous), it is God himself who does so, by "sending his own Son . . . " (v. 3). How exactly Christ's coming accomplishes salvation is not spelled out here, for what the apostle wants chiefly to emphasize is that freedom from the law means freedom from the "flesh" as well, and freedom for a wholly new existence in the Spirit (see v. 4). But life in the Spirit is nothing else than life in Christ, as the virtual identification of "the Spirit of God" and "the Spirit of Christ" (v. 9) suggests. Thus, the lection as presently framed closes, just as it opened, with a wonderfully liberating affirmation about the new life in Christ (v. 10): "But if Christ is in you, although your body is dead because of sin, the Spirit means life because of righteousness" (author's translation).

GOSPEL: MATTHEW 20:17-28

This lection consists of two separate pericopes, vv. 17-19 and vv. 20-28. These stand together in Mark as they do here in Matthew (Mark 10:32-34, followed by vv. 35-45), but in Luke they are separated by several chapters (Luke 18:31-34; 22:24-27).

Matthew, following Mark, portrays Jesus as issuing three solemn predictions about his forthcoming suffering, death, and resurrection. In the first part of our present lection (vv. 17-19) we have the last of these, the first two having appeared in 16:21 and 17:22-23. The parallel predictions in Mark (8:31; 9:31; 10:32-34) are a vital part of that evangelist's portrayal of Jesus as the "secret Messiah," whose mission as the suffering Son of man is only gradually disclosed to his followers. Here in Matthew these predictions are also used in the service of the evangelist's christology, underscoring the point that Jesus is present in the world as one whose destiny, under God, is to die and be resurrected for the sake of the world. Thus, the first of the Matthean predictions is introduced by the formula "From that time Jesus began to . . ." (16:21), repeated from 4:17, where it had introduced the beginning of Jesus' specific teaching, as he journeys toward Jerusalem, about his forthcoming death and resurrection.

Several characteristically Matthean touches are evident in the prediction included in our lection. The least important is this evangelist's use, in reference to Jesus' resurrection, of the phrase "*on* the third day" instead of Mark's "*after* three days." It is possible, but by no means certain, that this wording (found in all three Matthean predictions, in the Lucan parallels, and also in 1 Cor. 15:4) echoes Hos. 6:2 (see the First Lesson for this Sunday).

It is rather more significant that only Matthew—and then only in this third prediction—specifies that Jesus died by crucifixion (v. 19; contrast Mark's "kill"). However, what is most striking is the way this evangelist introduces the prediction (v. 17). In contrast to Mark's "And they [Jesus and his disciples] w ᷓe on the road, going up to Jerusalem . . . ," Matthew focuses attention on Jesus alone: "And as Jesus was going up to Jerusalem . . ." Moreover, in accord with his own more positive view of the disciples, Matthew omits Mark's references to the surprise and fear that gripped them as they followed Jesus on his way to the predicted suffering and death in Jerusalem.

Most of us would prefer to think of Jesus' disciples as Matthew tends to: as people eager to learn, quick to respond, ready to follow wherever Jesus goes. However, Mark's portrayal of them as slow to understand who Jesus is and what his mission is all about, and surprised that he would go up to Jerusalem, is probably closer to the historical truth. It is certainly closer to the truth about *us* as disciples: surprised not only at what Jesus does but at what he asks of us, reluctant to give up our old ways for his ways, fearful of what might happen to us should we indeed follow him "up to Jerusalem."

The kinder Matthean view of the disciples is also apparent in the way this evangelist tells the story that constitutes the remainder of our lection (vv. 20–28). According to Mark's account, James and John brazenly ask Jesus for privileged places in his future kingdom (Mark 10:35–37). However, according to Matthew (who refers to them only as "the sons of Zebedee") it is their mother who makes the request—even though from v. 22 on Jesus responds not to her but to the two brothers. Still, because the evangelist allows this story to retain its position immediately following the third passion prediction (as it does in Mark), the striking contrast between the selfish ambitions of these two disciples and the selfless behavior of Jesus is hardly diminished.

The popular hymn "Are Ye Able?" is based on this story of Jesus' conversation with the sons of Zebedee, and yet one must ask whether the words of the rousing chorus—"Lord, we are able, our spirits are thine"—do justice to the biblical text. One must observe, first, that the request made of Jesus—that James and John be granted places of honor in the coming kingdom—is turned back by Jesus. He replies, "You do not know what you are asking," and then he puts a question to *them:* "Are you able to drink the cup that I am to drink?" (v. 22a, b). The "cup" to which Jesus refers is of course the cup of suffering and death which he himself will pray to be spared (see Matt. 26:39, 42). Second, it would appear that these two disciples are so eager for the glory of the kingdom that they remain oblivious to the suffering that is to precede it, because in the context of this story their response to Jesus' query—"We are able" (v. 22c)—comes across as wholly naive. Third, it is important to notice that, while Jesus assures them that they will indeed suffer, he can make no promises about future rewards (v. 23). Neither power nor position can be guaranteed to those who follow Jesus—only suffering, for they are following one who is on his way "up to Jerusalem."

The sequel to this conversation, which comes in vv. 24–28, is built around the saying in vv. 26–27, to which the Son of man saying in v. 28 had already been added in Mark. The first of these, a saying about greatness, evidently circulated independently of this particular story, because another version of it is used in 23:11 (note the parallel in Mark 9:35, and compare Luke 9:48b). The evangelist probably wants his readers to interpret this saying as a word for the church as a whole, not just for James and John (contrast Mark 10:41–42). In contrast to what obtains among non-Christians ("the Gentiles," v. 25), within the church greatness is not to be defined with reference to power and position, but with reference to service (vv. 26–27).

Somehow we have allowed ourselves to become comfortable with this text, whereas it is in fact one of the most revolutionary sayings in the whole Synoptic tradition. It turns upside down what common sense and experience seem to require us to believe—that greatness inheres in the ability (whether of individuals, organizations, or governments) to exercise "authority" over others. It calls us to devote ourselves to caring for others, not to controlling them (whether by force of personality or by economic, political, or military power). This is supported by an appeal to the mission of Jesus himself, identified in v. 28 as "the Son of man who came not to be served but to serve, and to give his life as a ransom for many." The association here of Jesus' servant-mission with his sacrificial death recalls the portrayal of the Suffering Servant of God that one finds in Isaiah 53, to which this saying might possibly be indebted. But in the present context the saying is about discipleship as much as it is about Jesus. It is a call to the church to recognize, as James and John had not, that the most urgent question is not who will sit at Jesus' right hand and at his left in the kingdom, but who will walk and serve at his right hand and at his left as he makes his way "up to Jerusalem."

The Fifth Sunday in Lent

Lutheran	Roman Catholic	Episcopal	Pres/UCC/Chr	Meth/COCU
Ezek. 37:1–3 (4–10) 11–14	Ezek. 37:12–14	Ezek. 37:1–3 (4–10) 11–14	Ezek. 37:11–14	Ezek. 37:1–14
Rom. 8:11–19	Rom. 8:8–11	Rom. 6:16–23	Rom. 8:6–11	Rom. 8:6–19
John 11:1–53 or John 11:47–53	John 11:1–45 or John 11:3–7, 17, 20–27, 33–45	John 11:(1–17) 18–44	John 11:1–4, 17, 34–44	John 11:1–53

All three of the lessons for this Sunday speak of resurrection from the dead, although in rather different ways and for very different reasons. Ezekiel's vision of the dry bones concerns the Israelites who languish in Babylonian exile; the Johannine narrative about Lazarus's resurrection is presented as one of Jesus' "signs" and points on ahead to Jesus' own death and resurrection; and Paul's comments, which stand within the context of his appeals to walk by the Spirit, concern primarily the believer's future resurrection with Christ.

FIRST LESSON:
EZEKIEL 37:1–3 (4–10) 11–14

Here the prophet Ezekiel is addressing his fellow exiles in Babylon after 587 B.C. The utter despair and hopelessness that characterized the exilic community in those years is well expressed in v. 11 where Israel's own plaintive cry is quoted: "Our bones are dried up, and our hope is lost; we are clean cut off." The lament arises not only out of its humiliating experience of defeat and exile, but also from its sense that what has befallen constituted God's judgment upon its sins. Ezekiel's vision of the dry bones (vv. 1–10) evidently derives from this melancholy self-assessment. There is Israel, dead but not properly buried, its bones picked clean by the wild animals and birds of prey, and bleached white by the relentless sun. Withered and brittle, the exiles—like T. S. Eliot's "hollow men"—seem drained of anything like real life, trapped in a meaningless existence.

No human being is a stranger to feelings of despair and to the experience of meaningless. Thus, the question that God put to Ezekiel, "Can these bones live?" (v. 3a), is often on our lips, too. Ezekiel's response, however, is a bit surprising. Why doesn't he answer, Yes, O Lord, by thy mercy and power these bones can live, and then proceed to make an appeal on behalf of his people? Instead, the prophet says only, "O Lord God, thou knowest" (v. 3b). Everything is left to God; nothing is taken for granted about God's mercy. Thus, when God's Word comes to Ezekiel it is a genuine word of mercy, the expression of God's own purpose to save: the flesh will be restored to those dry bones, and Israel shall once again be filled with the breath of life (vv. 5–6).

The vision as such concludes with a description of the reassembling of the dry bones and their reconstitution as living beings (vv. 7–10).

The two phases of this restoration (vv. 8–10; cf. vv. 5–6) parallel the two-step creation of man as portrayed in Gen. 2:7—first the visible part, then the invisible breath of God which brings the creature of life. Israel may anticipate a *new* creation, and like the original one it will manifest the presence of the Creator: "And you shall know that I am the Lord" (v. 6). It is in that "knowledge"—in a renewed relationship to their Lord—that the exiles will be restored to life.

The interpretation of the vision comes in vv. 11–14, even though the imagery changes. Now one hears of corpses rather than of skeletons: "Thus says the Lord God: Behold, I will open your graves, O my people; and I will bring you home into the land of Israel" (v. 12). There is an allusion here to Israel's flight from Egypt into the promised land, and it invites the exiles to think of their impending deliverance and return as a new exodus. This will be an exodus not only from Babylon, but from fear and from despair; and it will be a return not only to their own land, but to their God. Indeed, the formula of v. 6 is repeated in v. 13, "And you shall know that I am the Lord. . . . " Israel's new life will in.olve a renewal of her vision of God, and of her identity as God's covenant people. This is reinforced when the promise is rephrased in the closing verse: "And I will put my Spirit within you, and you shall live . . . " (v. 14a).

What does it mean to have God's Spirit "within you"? How does the Spirit bring life? What kind of life is it that the Spirit makes possible? How Ezekiel might respond to such questions is suggested when we compare the wording of v. 14a with that of the similar promise in 36:27 (cf. 39:29): "And I will put my [S]pirit within you, and cause you to walk in my statutes and be careful to observe my ordinances." Here, as in most biblical texts, the Spirit is conceived, first of all, as God's presence within the whole community of faith—certainly not as the private possession of solitary individuals. The Spirit enlivens by enabling Israel to remain faithful to the obligations to the covenant by which she has been constituted as the people of God. Thus, the life that the Spirit makes possible is not necessarily marked by extraordinary "religious experiences" or distinctive "spiritual powers"; the single essential mark of the Spirit's presence is obedience to the will of God, within the context of the community of faith.

SECOND LESSON: ROMANS 8:11–19

The opening verse of this lection must be read in connection with Rom. 8:1–10, where Paul has written of the freedom and the responsibility that are given with the new life of the Spirit. For those who are open to the indwelling presence of Christ, he says, "the Spirit means life" (v. 10, author's translation). The apostle is thinking of the experience of meaning and purpose that believers have even while they remain subject to sin and death. However, the declaration that follows (v. 11), for which he is perhaps indebted to the tradition, points beyond the present to the future, beyond mortality to resurrection. Thus, even as it rounds off the comments in 8:1–10 it adds something to them— specifically, an affirmation that the freedom in which the believer presently lives will be extended to include deliverance from the limitations inherent to mortality.

There are some more affirmations about the future fulfillment of God's gift of life in the following paragraph (vv. 14–17), but they are made primarily to support the appeals with which it opens (vv. 12–13). The last two verses of this lection (vv. 18–19) are best regarded as opening a new paragraph (see RSV), even though Paul's focus on the future continues through v. 25.

The appeals in vv. 12–13 derive from the discussion in vv. 1–11 and are based on that. Here we encounter another of the many instances in Paul's letters where indicatives form the basis for imperatives. Indeed, every one of Paul's indicative statements has an inherently imperative force. The affirmations in vv. 1–11 about "the Spirit of life in Christ Jesus" (v. 2) are simultaneously appeals to "walk according to the Spirit" (see vv. 4, 5). Galatians 5:25 makes the connection that is implicit here quite explicit in a classically Pauline indicative/ imperative formulation: "If we live by the Spirit, let us also walk by the Spirit."

In vv. 12–17 the apostle employs several images in order to help his readers understand what faith properly involves. The first, which portrays believers as "debtors," is not developed because Paul interrupts himself, and the sentence in which it is introduced (v. 12) is never completed (v. 13 moves to a new thought). Clearly, however, what the apostle had started out to say was that his readers should think of themselves as "debtors, not to the flesh, to live according to the flesh" (v. 12), but as debtors to the Spirit, to live according to the Spirit. The use of this image certainly is not meant to evoke the corresponding image of God as a heavenly creditor who expects payment for services rendered. After all, Paul has written of the Holy Spirit as that "which has been *given* to us," and through which God's love has been "poured into our hearts" (Rom. 5:5). What God has bestowed without regard to merit (see Rom. 5:6–11) is surely not given with the expectation of subsequent payment.

Then in what sense does Paul think of believers as "debtors" to the Spirit? Perhaps the clue is to be found in the injunction of Rom. 13:8: "Owe no one anything, except to love one another; for he who loves his neighbor has fulfilled the law." To be indebted to the Spirit means to be indebted to God's love, by which one's life has been graced and through which one has been drawn into a community of faith. Because God's love remains a gift, freely bestowed and unmerited, this debt is one that can never be paid off. Believers are nonetheless accountable for their stewardship of God's gift of love. Their faith—their trusting reception of God's love—is to find concrete expression in their own acts of love (Gal. 5:6). For Paul, walking "according to the Spirit" is nothing else than "walking in love" toward one another (Rom. 14:15), whereby the community of faith is built up (see 1 Cor. 8:1). This is why he writes that the obligation to love one another should be one's only debt, and why he understands this to be a continuing, never-ending debt, even as God's "love never ends" (1 Cor. 13:8). It is a debt that is never stamped "Paid in Full," for on this account the books are never closed.

A second image that deserves attention appears in vv. 14–16. Here Paul refers to believers as God's "sons" (v. 14) and, more inclusively, as God's "children" (v. 16). The corresponding image of God as a parent, specifically, as Father, is certainly in the apostle's mind (see v. 15). To portray believers as God's "children" or "sons" is to suggest that they have their very being in God, and that any attempt to deny or to renounce their dependence on God not only breaks a vital relationship but violates their own nature.

The "genealogy" of the Christian community is sketched in Rom. 9:7–8. Paul insists that Abraham's true descendants, and therefore

God's true children, are not "children of the flesh," those who seek to live out of their own frail, human resources. Rather, God's true children are "the children of the promise," those who, like Abraham (Romans 4), place their trust in God's power to give the life for which they yearn, but which they cannot themselves create. Thus, Paul reminds the Galatians that "in Christ Jesus [they] are all sons of God through faith" (Gal 3:26), and in the lection before us he reminds the Romans that it is by the leading of the Spirit that they are God's sons (v. 14). He adds that their acclamation of God as "Abba! Father!"—perhaps a familiar part of the baptismal liturgy—confirms this, because it could have been prompted only by the Spirit (vv. 16–17).

When we meet strangers, the first two questions we usually ask are, What is your name? and Where are you from? Their answers disclose a good deal about who they understand themselves to be. Similarly, when Christians present themselves as "children of God" they are declaring to whose family they belong, as well as from whom they have come. However, because the family with which they identify themselves is the family of *God,* it is not just one family among others, but the entire *human* family. To call God one's parent is to embrace and to care for every stranger as one's "sister" or "brother." The church's world mission and its passion for social justice are fundamental to its life—and absolutely inseparable—precisely because it is from this conviction that they both derive.

In his portrayal of believers as debtors and as children, Paul is thinking of how their present lives bear the marks of what God has done and of who God has been for them. When he expands the second of these to include the idea of believers as "heirs" (v. 17), his vision of faith's present is enlarged to encompass its future as well. If we are God's children, he says, then we are "heirs of God and fellow heirs with Christ." This image receives its fullest development in Galatians 3 and 4, where the apostle declares that by baptism into Christ believers become "Abraham's offspring" and, with him, "heirs according to promise" (Gal. 3:28–29). The promise given to Abraham was that through his faith the Gentiles would be blessed (Gal. 3:8–9). Paul describes this further as "the promise of faith" (Gal. 3:14), and he identifies it closely with the gospel of Christ (Gal. 3:8). To understand oneself as heir to this promise is to recognize that God's purpose will find its fulfillment only in God's own future, and that God's future must be allowed to claim and transform one's present life. An heir is one who has yet to receive the inheritance, but who is already a new person by reason of what is still to come. Typically, Paul describes the inheritance of believers only in general terms, and most often as their being "glorified [with Christ]," as in v. 17 of our lection (see also vv. 18, 30). Once, however, he describes it rather more specifically as "the glorious liberty of the children of God" (v. 21), probably a reference to the perfect freedom they shall experience when all things have been subjected to the Father, that "God may be everything to every one" (1 Cor. 15:28). But this freedom that awaits believers when they inherit God's kingdom is already present, in part, to faith. It is one portion of the down payment on the future inheritance that believers receive when the Spirit is given (2 Cor. 1:22; 5:5), for "where the Spirit of the Lord is, there is freedom" (2 Cor. 3:17). The present gift of freedom is also in view in Gal. 4:1–7, where Paul contrasts a householder's heirs, free to receive the inheritance, with the household slave who will inherit nothing (see also Gal. 4:30–31).

Finally, it is important to consider what the apostle means when he describes believers as "fellow heirs with Christ" (Rom. 8:17). We naturally think first of sharing in Christ's resurrection life, or of finding a seat at his right hand or at his left in his kingdom. How glorious the prospect! But the text surprises us, as biblical texts often do. We are only "fellow heirs with Christ," says Paul, *"provided we suffer* with him. . . ." There is no Easter without Good Friday— not for Jesus, and not for those who would be his followers. For to be baptized into Christ means to be baptized into his death (Rom. 6:3), and to be baptized into his death means to die to one's old self (Rom. 6:6; 2 Cor. 5:15) and to "walk in newness of life" (Rom. 6:4). That, finally, is what Paul means by walking "according to the Spirit" (Rom. 8:4), because it is to the Spirit, "not to the flesh," that we are all—and always—debtors (Rom. 8:12).

GOSPEL: JOHN 11:1–53 (or 11:47–53)

We shall misunderstand this passage if we approach it assuming that it is primarily a story about the raising of Lazarus from the dead, and if our main question is about what "really" happened. Like every other Johannine narrative it is fundamentally a story about Jesus, and the main questions with which we should approach it are, How does it fit into the overall structure of the Fourth Gospel? and What meaning does the evangelist want his readers to find in it? This narrative is, indeed, both distinctively Johannine (it stands in no other Gospel) and characteristically Johannine (in the way it is told and in what is said).

Within the overall structure of the Gospel of John, this incident serves, first of all, as one of several "signs" pointing to Jesus. In particular, the evangelist employs this story of the death and resurrection of Lazarus to point his readers on ahead to Jesus' own death and resurrection. A hint of this comes when Jesus says, "This illness is not unto death; it is for the glory of God, so that the Son of God may be glorified by means of it" (v. 4). In this Gospel, references to Jesus' "glorification" are references to his death (see, e.g., 7:39), since the Fourth Evangelist conceives of Jesus' being "lifted up" on the cross as his being "lifted up," simultaneously, in glory (see, e.g., 12:32–33).

If the remark in v. 4 is not enough of a hint, then the epilogue in vv. 45–53 leaves no question about the evangelist's intent. Not only has the incident at Bethany prompted the Sanhedrin to plan for Jesus' execution; in the midst of its deliberations Caiaphas, quite unwittingly, comes very close to articulating a Christian interpretation of the benefits of Jesus' death (v. 50). And just in case the double meaning is too subtle for readers to catch, the evangelist spells it out quite explicitly: "[Caiaphas] did not say this of his own accord, but being high priest that year he prophesied that Jesus should die for the nation, and not for the nation only, but to gather into one the children of God who are scattered abroad" (vv. 51–52).

This story, then, provides not only an awesome climax for the series of signs the Fourth Evangelist has presented, beginning with the account of the wedding at Cana (2:1–11). It also offers a dramatic preview of what Jesus himself will experience when he journeys to Jerusalem for the impending Passover (11:55). But there is still more. The sign itself—Lazarus's resurrection—must not be viewed in isolation from the preceding scenes which show Jesus conversing with Lazarus's sisters, first with Martha and then with Mary.

Nothing is gained by trying to compare the characterization of these two women in Luke 10:38–42 with the way they are portrayed in the present narrative. It is true that Martha seems to be the more "active" and "practical" one in both stories—in Luke, busily engaged as hostess while Mary attends to Jesus' teaching; here in John, the first to welcome Jesus while Mary sits at home. However, it is clear from the dialogue that the Fourth Evangelist wants us to regard Martha, not Mary, as the one who *really* attends to Jesus' word, and who is, therefore, the model of the true believer. The fact that Martha and Mary speak exactly the same words in greeting Jesus (note vv. 21 and 32) suggests that the narrator wants us to compare the two conversations. And when we do, we notice what a different course each of them takes.

The greeting, spoken first by Martha (v. 21), is in fact a gentle reprimand: "Lord, if you had been here, my brother would not have died." Yet Martha indicates by her actions—she has left the house to meet Jesus—as well as by her further comment, "and even now I know that whatever you ask from God, God will give you," that she still expects something from Jesus. What she receives from him is the promise that Lazarus "will rise again." Her reply, "I know that he will rise again in the resurrection at the last day" (v. 24), suggests that she understands Jesus to mean only that Lazarus, in accord with traditional Pharisaic doctrine, will participate in the general resurrection at some future, but indeterminate, date. Yes, she clings to that hope, too. But no, Jesus means something else. He is not there to console her with a hope for something that is yet to come; he is there to confront her with what is already a reality: "I am the resurrection and the life" (v. 25). It is on this, a typically Johannine "I am" saying, that the whole of the narrative centers. This pronouncement, not Lazarus's rather ludicrous stumbling out of the tomb (v. 44a), is the climactic moment of Jesus' visit to Bethany.

The life of which Jesus speaks here is to be identified with that which is described elsewhere in this Gospel as "eternal life." The Fourth Evangelist does not conceive eternal life quantitatively, as the indefinite prolongation of one's physical existence. Rather, he conceives it qualitatively, as life no longer held hostage by the fears, anxieties, and desperate ambitions that so often control and, finally, dehumanize us. For this evangelist, eternal life comes in one's "hearing" Jesus' word and "believing" the one who sent him (5:24). Since Jesus was sent on a mission of love (e.g., 3:16; 13:1), and since his word is to be heard as the "new commandment" to love one another (cf. 12:48–50 with 13:34), eternal life in the Johannine sense consists of receiving God's love as it is present in Jesus (cf. 17:3) and accepting one's own role as a missioner of love in the world (cf. 17:18 with 17:22–23). We may assume that all of this is involved when Jesus challenges Martha with the question, "Do you believe this?" (v. 26), and when she answers, "Yes, Lord; I believe that you are the Christ, the Son of God, he who is coming into the world" (v. 27).

Note: Lazarus still lies dead in the tomb. There has not yet been any sign, only Jesus' word. Without having seen, Martha believes; and thereby she becomes one of those upon whom the final beatitude of this Gospel is pronounced (20:29b).

Martha, at Jesus' bidding, summons her sister Mary—who has remained in the house all the time (v. 28). In greeting Jesus, Mary repeats verbatim Martha's gentle reprimand (v. 32); but, apparently expecting nothing from Jesus, she returns immediately to her mourning (v. 33). Jesus is indignant and troubled that she and "the Jews" (who in this Gospel regularly stand for all unbelievers) are so consumed by their grieving that they are not open to the word of life that he brings (v. 33b). This is why Jesus weeps (v. 35)—not out of his love for Lazarus, as the Jews mistakenly presume (v. 36), but out of sorrow for their indifference to the life that is present in their midst. This indifference prompts Jesus to ask where Lazarus is entombed, and then, going there, to perform a sign. In this case as in others, the evangelist seems to want us to recognize that Jesus is offering the sign only as a concession to unbelief (note v. 42).

What is the outcome of all of this? In a later scene we find Lazarus and his sisters entertaining Jesus at supper (12:1–8). Since on that occasion Mary anoints Jesus' feet with a costly ointment (12:3), it is implied that she had been moved to believe in Jesus because of her brother's resurrection. Martha, who had believed in Jesus' word even before that sign, is serving (12:2). And what of Lazarus himself? That he, too, became a believer seems to be implied when the narrator later remarks that "on account of him many Jews were going away [from their synagogues?] and believing" (12:11). Ironically, however,

Lazarus is once more in mortal danger (12:10)—which confirms that the eternal life experienced by one who believes in Jesus (see 11:25–26a) has to do with the quality of one's present existence, and not with indefinite physical survival.

Beyond this, we are told nothing about what happened to Lazarus or to his sisters. Perhaps that is because the evangelist's chief concern is with what can happen to his *readers* when *they* respond to Jesus' life-giving word and presence. Because he is present as God's love incarnate, to believe in him means to receive his love; and because his word is the new commandment to love one another, to be his disciples means to be "discipled" to a service of love in the world. For believers he is indeed "the resurrection and the life," because through his presence and his word they are enlivened with a purpose that transcends and transforms their mortal existence.